200 Ligh

healthy curries

200 Light
healthy curries

hamlyn **all color**

An Hachette UK Company
www.hachette.co.uk

First published in Great Britain in 2015 by Hamlyn
a division of Octopus Publishing Group Ltd
Endeavour House, 189 Shaftesbury Avenue
London WC2H 8JY
www.octopusbooks.co.uk

Distributed in the US by Hachette Book Group
1290 Avenue of the Americas, 4th and 5th Floors
New York, NY 10020

Distributed in Canada by Canadian Manda Group
664 Annette St.,Toronto, Ontario, Canada M6S 2C8

ISBN: 978-0-60062-969-6
Printed and bound in China.

10 9 8 7 6 5 4 3 2 1

Standard level kitchen cup and spoon measurements are
used in all recipes

Ovens should be preheated to the specified temperature;
if using a convection oven, follow the manufacturer's
instructions for adjusting the time and temperature.

Fresh herbs, large eggs, and freshly ground black pepper
should be used unless otherwise stated.

This book includes dishes made with nuts and nut
derivatives. It is advisable for people with known allergic
reactions to nuts and nut derivatives or those who may be
potentially vulnerable to these allergies, such as pregnant
and nursing mothers, people with a weakened immune sys-
tem, the elderly, babies, and children, to avoid dishes made
with these. It is prudent to check the labels of all prepared
ingredients for the possible inclusion of nut derivatives.

contents

introduction

introduction

this series

The Hamlyn All Color Light Series is a collection of in handy, compact books, each packed with more than 200 healthy recipes on a variety of topics and cuisines to suit your needs.

The books are designed to help those people who are trying to lose weight by offering a range of delicious recipes that are low in calories but still high in flavor. The recipes show a calorie count per portion, so you will know exactly what you are eating. These are recipes for real and delicious food, not ultra-dieting meals, so they will help you maintain your new healthier eating plan for life. They must be used as part of a balanced diet, with the cakes and sweet dishes eaten only as an occasional treat.

how to use this book

All the recipes in this book are clearly marked with the number of calories (cal) per serving. The chapters cover different calorie bands: Under 500 calories, under 400 calories, etc.

Many recipes have variations at the bottom of the page; note the calorie count because they do vary and can sometimes be more than the original recipe.

The figures assume that you are using low-fat versions of dairy products, so be sure to use skimd milk and low-fat yogurt. They have also been calculated using lean meat, so make sure you trim meat of all visible fat and remove the skin from chicken breasts. Use moderate amounts of oil and butter for cooking and low-fat/low-calorie alternatives when you can.

Don't forget to take note of the number of servings each recipe makes and divide up the quantity of food accordingly, so that you know just how many calories you are consuming.

Be careful about side dishes and accompaniments that will also add to the calorie content.

Above all, enjoy trying out the new flavors and exciting recipes that this book contains. Instead of dwelling on the thought that you are denying yourself your usual unhealthy treats, think of your new program as a positive step toward a new you. Not only will you lose weight and feel more confident, but your health will benefit, the condition of your hair and nails will improve, and you will take on a healthy glow.

the risks of obesity

Up to half of all women and two-thirds of men are overweight or obese in the developed world today. Being overweight can not only make us unhappy with our appearance, but can also lead to serious health problems, including heart disease, high blood pressure, and diabetes.

When someone is obese, it means they are overweight to the point that it could start to seriously threaten their health. In fact, obesity ranks as a close second to smoking as a possible cause of cancer. Obese women are more at risk of having complications during and after pregnancy, and people who are overweight or obese are also more at risk of experiencing coronary heart disease, gallstones, osteoarthritis, high blood pressure, and type 2 diabetes.

how can I tell if I am overweight?

The best way to tell if you are overweight is to work out your body mass index (BMI). If using U.S. standard measurements, divide your weight in pounds (lb) by your height in inches (in) squared and multiply by 703. (For example, if you are 5 feet 4 inches, or 64 inches, tall and you weigh 130 pounds, the calculation would be $130 \div 64^2$ (or 4,096) $= 0.0317 \times 703 = 22.3$.) If using metric measurements, divide your weight in kilograms (kg) by your height in meters (m) squared. Then compare the figure to the following list (these figures apply only to healthy adults).

Less than 20	underweight
20–25	healthy
25–30	overweight
Over 30	obese

As we all know by now, one of the major causes of obesity is eating too many calories.

what is a calorie?

Our bodies need energy to stay alive, grow, keep warm, and be active. We get the energy we need to survive from the food and beverages we consume—more specifically, from the fat, carbohydrate, protein, and alcohol that they contain.

A calorie (cal), as anyone who has ever been on a diet will know, is the unit used to measure how much energy different foods contain. A calorie can be scientifically defined as the energy required to raise the temperature of 1 gram of water from 58°F to 60°F. A kilocalorie (kcal) is 1,000 calories and although we refer to calories (cal), it is, in fact, kilocalories that we usually mean when we talk about the calories in different foods.

Different food types contain different numbers of calories. For example, a gram of carbohydrate (starch or sugar) provides 3.75 cal, protein provides 4 cal per gram, fat provides 9 cal per gram ,and alcohol provides 7 cal per gram. So, fat is the most concentrated source of energy—weight for weight, it provides just over twice as many calories as either protein or carbohydrate—

with alcohol not far behind. The energy content of a food or drink depends on how many grams of carbohydrate, fat, protein, and alcohol are present.

how many calories do we need?

The number of calories we need to consume varies from person to person, but your body weight is a clear indication of whether you are eating the right amount. Body weight is simply determined by the number of calories you are eating compared to the number of calories your body is using to maintain itself and needed for physical activity. If you regularly consume more calories than you use up, you will start to gain weight, because extra energy is stored in the body as fat.

Based on our relatively inactive modern-day lifestyles, most nutritionists recommend that women should aim to consume around

2,000 calories (cal) per day, and men an amount of about 2,500. Of course, the amount of energy required depends on your level of activity: the more active you are, the more energy you need to maintain a stable weight.

a healthier lifestyle

To maintain a healthy body weight, we need to expend as much energy as we eat; to lose weight, energy expenditure must, therefore, exceed intake of calories. So, exercise is a vital tool in the fight to lose weight. Physical activity doesn't just help us control body weight; it also helps to reduce our appetite and is known to have beneficial effects on the heart and blood that help prevent against cardiovascular disease.

Many of us claim we don't enjoy exercise and simply don't have the time to fit it into our hectic schedules. So the easiest way to increase physical activity is by incorporating it into our daily routines, perhaps by walking or cycling instead of driving (particularly for short journeys), taking up more active hobbies, such as gardening, and taking small and simple steps, such as using the stairs instead of the elevator whenever possible.

As a general guide, adults should aim to undertake at least 30 minutes of moderate-intensity exercise, such as a brisk walk, five times a week. The 30 minutes does not have to be taken all at once: three sessions of 10 minutes are equally beneficial. Children and young people should be encouraged to take at least 60 minutes of moderate-intensity exercise every day.

Some activities will use up more energy than others. The following list shows some examples of the energy a person weighing 132 lb (60 kg) would expend doing the following activities for 30 minutes:

activity	energy
ironing	69 cal
cleaning	75 cal
walking	99 cal
golf	129 cal
fast walking	150 cal
cycling	180 cal
aerobics	195 cal
swimming	195 cal
running	300 cal
sprinting	405 cal

make changes for life

The best way to lose weight is to try to adopt healthier eating habits that you can easily maintain all the time, not just when you are trying to become thinner. Aim to lose no more than 2 lb (1 kg) per week to be sure you lose only your fat stores. People who go on crash diets lose lean muscle as well as fat and will be much more prone to putting the weight back on again soon afterward.

For a woman, the aim is to reduce her daily calorie intake to around 1,500 cal while she is trying to lose weight, then settle on around 2,000 per day thereafter to maintain her new body weight. Regular exercise will also make a huge difference: the more you can burn, the less you will need to diet.

improve your diet

For most of us, simply adopting a more balanced diet will reduce our calorie intake and lead to weight loss. Follow these simple recommendations:

Eat more starchy foods, such as bread, potatoes, rice, and pasta. Assuming these replace the fattier foods you usually eat, and you don't smother them with oil or butter, this will help reduce the amount of fat and increase the amount of fiber in your diet. As a bonus, try to use whole-grain rice, pasta, and flour, because the energy from these foods is released more slowly in the body, making you feel fuller for longer.

Eat more fruit and vegetables, aiming for at least five portions of different fruit and vegetables a day (excluding potatoes).

As long as you don't add extra fat to your fruit and vegetables in the form of cream, butter, or oil, these changes will help reduce your fat intake and increase the amount of fiber and vitamins you consume.

who said vegetables must be dull?

Eat fewer sugary foods, such as cookies, cakes, and chocolate candy. This will also help reduce your fat intake. If you want something sweet, choose fresh or dried fruit instead.

Reduce the amount of fat in your diet, so you consume fewer calories. Low-fat versions are available for most dairy products, including milk, cheese, sour cream, yogurt, and even cream and butter. Choose these instead of whole-fat versions; it doesn't necessarily mean your food will be tasteless.

Choose lean meat, such as Canadian-style bacon instead of fatty bacon, and chicken breasts instead of thighs. Trim all visible fat off meat before cooking and avoid frying foods— broil or roast instead. Fish is naturally low in fat and can make a variety of tempting dishes.

simple steps to reduce your intake

Few of us have an iron will, so when you are trying to cut down, make it easier on yourself by following these steps:

- Give yourself small servings to start with. You may feel satisfied when you have finished, but if you are still hungry you can always go back for more.
- Once you have served your meal, put away any leftover food before you eat. Don't put piled-up serving dishes on the table, as you will undoubtedly pick, even if you feel satisfied with what you have already eaten.
- Eat slowly and savor your food; then you will more probably feel full when you have finished. If you rush a meal, you may still feel hungry afterward.
- Make an effort with your meals. Just because you are cutting down doesn't mean your meals have to be low on taste as well as calories. You will feel more satisfied with a meal you have really enjoyed and will be less likely to look for comfort in a bag of potato chips or a bar of chocolate.
- Plan your meals in advance to make sure you have all the ingredients you need. Hunting around in the kitchen cabinets when you are hungry is unlikely to result in a healthy, balanced meal.
- Keep healthy and interesting snacks on hand for those moments when you need something to pep you up. You don't need to succumb to a candy bar if there are other tempting treats available.

curries

Originating from the South Indian Tamil word *kari*, which means gravy or sauce, the word "curry" literally refers to the spice blend used to flavor a dish. The word has evolved to describe a wide variety of saucy, spiced dishes from all over India, Southeast Asia, and even as far as Japan. We once used the word to describe an entire cuisine, but recently we have begun to discover the true diversity of a favorite food, and we are being introduced to authentic recipes from the many countries that provide spicy dishes that fall under the "curry" umbrella.

A common perception is that a curry is a hot and spicy dish. Yes, you can eat a curry that will blow your socks off but, on the whole, most curry recipes are delicate and highly sophisticated, containing a balanced blend of spices and herbs.

As food lovers today, we have embraced curries from all over the world and count them among our favorite foods. There is nothing more satisfying to me than producing a rich, aromatic curry to share with friends and family.

Whatever its origins, a curry usually has a selection of fresh and dried herbs and spices. Depending on the dish, other ingredients could include chiles, curry leaves, ginger, garlic, shallots, lemon grass, coconut milk, palm sugar, tamarind paste, Thai fish sauce, shrimp paste, and diced tomatoes. The recipes and ingredients vary from region to region, as well as from country to country.

As knowledgeable and passionate food lovers today, we have embraced curries from all over the world. You can a number of the ingredients in a large supermarket, but with the miracle of Internet shopping, you can order exotic ingredients and have them delivered to your door.

This book offers exciting recipes to suit every palate, and you may soon find that you have joined the ranks of millions of curry addicts around the world.

healthy favorites

Unfortunately, many curries contain a lot of oil, butter, and cream, which are blended with herbs and spices to create rich but unhealthy dishes. The delicious recipes in this book will show you that you can cook healthy curries without compromising on flavor and taste.

We have re-created favorite traditional curries—and some more unusual ones—without relying on unhealthy ingredients. We use these in much smaller quantities than usual and replace them with healthier options, such as peanut oil, which is much lower in saturated fat than ghee, sunflower oil, or butter. We have used fat-free plain yogurt and reduced-fat coconut milk instead of cream and butter.

We have also omitted or reduced sugar and replaced it with agave syrup. Sweeter than honey, this organic, fat-free sweetener can replace sugar in many recipes—you only need a very small amount. Likewise, when seasoning your dishes, be sure to use salt sparingly, because a high intake can contribute to high blood pressure and heart disease.

basic ingredients

You can buy many of the ingredients you need for the recipes in this book in a large supermarket. Markets and ethnic food stores are great places to find the more unusual items, and they often stock large packages of spices at good prices. You can also order "exotic" ingredients from gourmet food and speciality Web sites and have them delivered.

dry spices

The flavor of dry spices decreases with time, so buy them in smaller quantities and use them quickly for best results.

amchoor

Dried mango powder, used as a souring agent in Indian curries. Substitute with a little lemon juice or tamarind paste if unavailable.

asafetida

Also known as devil's dung, this plant resin can be bought in a lump or dried and ground in powder form. It is strong in flavor. Usually used in tiny amounts in lentil dishes, it is believed to counteract flatulence.

cardamom

This is usually used whole, in its pod, as an aromatic to flavor rice and curries. You can also use the little black seeds inside the pods on their own by crushing them and using as part of a spice mixture or for a garam masala.

cassia

Also known as Chinese cinnamon, cassia is a type of aromatic tree bark; it can be bought as sticks, rolled bark or in powder form. It has a coarser texture and stronger flavor than cinnamon does.

chile

Whole dried red chiles add the fiery heat to a curry. Dried red pepper flakes tend to have a milder flavor and chili powders made from ground dried chiles vary in heat, ranging from mild or medium to hot.

cinnamon

This sweet and warming aromatic spice comes from the bark of a tree and is available as sticks or rolled bark. It is also widely used in ground powder form.

cloves

These aromatic dried buds from an evergreen tree can be used whole or ground to a powder.

coriander seeds

The small, pale brown seeds of the coriander plant have a fresh, citrus flavor. Available whole or ground, they form the base of many curry pastes and dry spice mixes.

cumin

Essential in Asian cooking, these small elongated brown seeds are used whole or ground, and have a distinctive, warm, pungent aroma. Whole seeds may be dry-roasted and sprinkled over a dish just before serving.

curry powders

Store-bought prepared curry powders are widely available and there are many different varieties, depending on the spice mix. Some are simply labeled as mild, medium, or hot, but there are many specific mixes, such as Tandoori Spice Mix or Madras Curry Powder.

fennel seeds

These small, pale green seeds have a subtle anise flavor and are used as a flavoring in some spice mixes.

fenugreek seeds

Usually square in shape, these tiny, shiny yellow seeds are used widely in pickles and ground into spice mixes for curries.

garam masala

This common spice mix is usually added to a dish at the end of cooking time. A classic garam masala mix comprises cardamom, cloves, cumin, peppercorns, cinnamon, and nutmeg. See page 80 for recipe.

mustard seeds

Black, brown, or yellow, these tiny round seeds are widely used as a flavoring to dishes and are usually fried in oil until they "pop" to impart a mellow, nutty flavor.

nigella seeds

Also known as black onion seeds or *kalonji*, these tiny, mat black, oval seeds are most frequently used to flavor breads and pickles.

saffron

These deep orange strands are the dried stamens from a particular type of crocus and are used to give rice dishes and desserts a musky fragrance and golden color.

star anise

These dark brown, flower-shape seed pods have a decidedly aniselike flavor.

turmeric

This bright yellow-orange rhizome is widely available as a dried, ground powder. Turmeric has a warm, musky flavor and is used in small quantities to add flavor and color to lentil and rice dishes and curries.

fresh herbs & aromatics

chiles

Fresh green and red chiles are used in many types of curries to provide heat and flavor. Much of the heat resides in the pith and seeds, so if you want to enjoy the chile taste with less heat, make a long slit down the length of the chile and carefully scrape out and discard the pith and seeds before slicing or chopping the flesh.

cilantro

The parsley of the East, fresh cilantro is used widely in Asian cooking. Often the delicate leaves are used to flavor dishes, but the stems and roots can also be used, especially in Thai curry pastes.

curry leaves

These highly aromatic leaves are used fresh in Indian and Southeast Asian cooking. They come attached to stems in sprays and are pulled off the stems before use. Fresh curry leaves freeze well and can be used straight from the freezer.

galangal

This rhizome is used in savory dishes in the same way as its cousin, ginger. It is peeled and cut into fine slivers or finely chopped. You can use fresh ginger root instead if you can't find any galangal.

garlic

One of the essential flavors used in cooking all over the world, garlic cooked with ginger and onion forms the base of many curries. It is used sliced, crushed, or grated.

ginger

Another indispensable aromatic, fresh root ginger has a fresh, peppery flavor and is used in both savory and sweet dishes.

kaffir lime leaves

The leaves from the knobbly kaffir lime are

highly aromatic. When used in a curry, they are usually finely shredded but are also sometimes left whole. They freeze well and can be used straight from the freezer.

lemon grass

Known as *sere* in Indonesia, *serai* in Malaysia, *takrai* in Thailand, and *tanglad* in the Phillipines, this green grass is used for its citrus flavor and aroma. It can be used whole by bruising the base of the stalk, or can be finely sliced or chopped. Remove the tough outer leaves before slicing or chopping, as they can be particularly fibrous.

onions

This humble vegetable forms the base of many curries. Sliced or chopped, it is usually slowly fried before the other ingredients are added. Store onions in a wire basket in the kitchen at room temperature.

shallots

These small, sweet, and pungent members of the onion family are widely used in Southeast Asian cooking. To peel them, slice them in half and only then remove the outer skin.

Thai basil

Found in Asian food stores, this delicate herb is used to garnish and flavor curries. You can substitute regular basil if you cannot find any.

other useful ingredients

chickpea flour

Also known as besan or gram flour, this pale yellow flour, made from dried chickpeas, is used for thickening and binding, as well as being the main ingredient in savory batters.

coconut milk & coconut cream

Widely used in Asian cooking, coconut milk is added to curries to impart a rich, creamy texture. For a healthier option, use reduced-fat coconut milk if you can find it. Coconut cream is a thicker, richer version that is also higher in fat. It is available is Asian stores and online—don't confuse it with sugar-filled cream of coconut used in beverages.

palm sugar

Known as *jaggery* in India and *nam tan peep* in Thailand, this sugar is produced from the sap of various kinds of palms. Sold in cakes or cans, palm sugar has a deep, caramel flavor and is light brown. It is used in curries to balance the spices. Use any brown sugar as a substitute.

shrimp paste

Also known as *kapee*, this is a pungent preserve used in Asian cooking. Made by pounding shrimp with salt and letting it decompose, it has a powerful aroma that disappears when cooked.

sweet chili sauce

This sweet and mild sauce is made from red chiles, sugar, garlic, and vinegar.

tamarind paste

Used as a souring agent in curries, the paste from the tamarind pod can be used straight from the jar. You can also buy it in semidried pulp form, which needs to be soaked in warm water and strained before use.

Thai fish sauce

Also known as *nam pla*, this sauce is made from the liquid extracted from salted, fermented fish and is one of the main ingredients in Thai cooking.

recipes
under 200
calories

mandarin & litchi frappé

Calories per serving **68**
Makes **⅔ cup**

⅓ cup canned **mandarin oranges (tangerines)** in natural juice
¼ cup canned **litchis** in natural juice
ice cubes

Put the oranges and litchis and their juices into a food processor or blender, add the ice cubes, and process briefly.

Pour the frappé into glasses and serve immediately.

For ruby smoothie, put the juice of 2 oranges and 1 apple in a food processor or blender with 1¼ cups raspberries and 1 cup hulled strawberries. Add ⅔ cup low fat yogurt and process briefly.
Calories per serving 241

seafood with chiles

Calories per serving **174**
Serves **4**
Preparation time **5 minutes**
Cooking time **about**
   10 minutes

1½ tablespoons **sunflower oil**
3–4 **garlic cloves**, finely
   chopped
1 **red bell pepper**, seeded
   and cut into bite-size pieces
1 **small onion**, cut into eighths
1 **carrot**, cut into matchsticks
14½ oz **prepared mixed
   seafood**, such as shrimp,
   squid, small scallops
1 inch piece of **fresh ginger
   root**, peeled and finely
   grated
2 tablespoons **vegetable** or
   seafood stock or **broth**
1 tablespoon **oyster sauce**
½ tablespoon **light soy sauce**
1 **long fresh red chile,**
   trimmed, seeded, and
   sliced diagonally
1–2 **scallions**, finely sliced

Heat the oil in a nonstick wok or skillet and stir-fry
the garlic over medium heat until it is lightly browned.

Add the red bell pepper, onion, and carrot and stir-fry
for 2 minutes.

Add all the seafood together with the ginger, stock
or broth, oyster sauce, and soy sauce and stir-fry for
2–3 minutes or until the shrimp turn pink and all the
seafood is cooked.

Add the chile and scallions and mix well together.
Spoon onto a serving plate and serve immediately,
with rice, if desired.

For seafood with pineapple sweet chile, stir-fry the
red bell pepper, onion, and carrot after the garlic has
lightly browned. Add all the seafood, ginger, stock, oyster
sauce, and 2–3 tablespoons pineapple-flavored sweet
chili sauce (or plain if the flavored version is unavailable).
Omit the scallion and add a handful of Thai basil leaves
with the chile, lightly toss together for a minute to
combine before serving. **Calories per serving 209**

malaysian spicy cauliflower

Calories per serving **118**
Serves **4**
Preparation time **10 minutes**
Cooking time **10 minutes**

2 tablespoons **peanut oil**
1 **fresh red chile,** seeded and
   finely chopped
1 **onion**, thickly sliced
2 **garlic cloves**, chopped
1 teaspoon **salt**
3¾ cups **small cauliflower
   florets**

Heat the oil in a wok over high heat until the oil starts to shimmer. Add the chile, onion, and garlic and stir-fry for 1 minute.

Add the salt and cauliflower. Stir well to combine all the flavors, then sprinkle with 3 tablespoons water, cover, and steam for 3–4 minutes, until tender.

For spicy cauliflower soup, start the recipe as above, adding 2 peeled and diced red-skinned or Yukon gold potatoes with the cauliflower. Once all the flavors are tossed together, pour in 4¼ cups vegetable stock or borth. Simmer for 15 minutes, then blend until smooth. Serve with a drizzle of chili oil. **Calories per serving 186**

watermelon cooler

Calories per serving **101**
Makes 1¼ **cups**

3½ oz **watermelon**
   (about ⅔ cup when
   prepared)
3½ oz **strawberries**
(about ⅔ cup when prepared)
   ½ cup **water**
small handful of **mint** or
   tarragon leaves, plus extra
   to serve (optional)

Skin and seed the watermelon and chop the flesh into cubes. Hull the strawberries. Freeze the melon and strawberries until solid.

Put the frozen melon and strawberries into a food processor or blender, add the water and the mint or tarragon, and process until smooth.

Pour the mixture into 2 short glasses, decorate with mint or tarragon leaves, if desired, and serve immediately.

For melon & almond smoothie, process ⅔ cup frozen honeydew melon or cantaloupe flesh with ½ cup sweetened, chilled almond milk. **Calories per serving 48**

gujarati carrot salad

Calories per serving **104**
Serves **4**
Preparation time **10 minutes**
Cooking time **2–3 minutes**

4½ cups shredded **carrots**
 (about 1 lb)
¼ cup **lemon juice**
1 tablespoon **honey**
1 tablespoon **vegetable oil**
½ teaspoon **dried red
 pepper flakes**
2 teaspoons **black mustard
 seeds**
4 **curry leaves**
salt

Put the carrots into a serving bowl. Mix the lemon juice and honey together and pour the dressing over the carrots. Season with salt.

Heat the oil in a small saucepan and add the red pepper flakes, mustard seeds, and curry leaves. As soon as the mustard seeds start to "pop," remove the saucepan from the heat and pour the mixture over the carrots. Stir well to mix.

For beet & carrot salad, replace half of the shredded carrots with 5 peeled and shredded freshly cooked beets and proceed as above. **Calories per serving 118**

cabbage bhaji

Calories per serving **110**
Serves **4**
Preparation time **10 minutes**
Cooking time **10 minutes**

5 cups coarsely chopped
   green cabbage (about 1 lb)
⅔ cup **boiling water**
1 tablespoon **vegetable oil**
2 teaspoons **urad dhal**
   (dried lentils)
1 teaspoon **black mustard
   seeds**
1 **dried red chile,** finely
   chopped
6–8 **curry leaves**
2 tablespoons **grated fresh
   coconut**
salt and **black pepper**

Put the cabbage into a large saucepan with the water, cover, and cook over medium heat for 10 minutes, stirring occasionally. Drain, return to the pan, set aside, and keep warm.

Meanwhile, heat the oil in a small nonstick skillet and add the urad dhal, mustard seeds, and chile. Stir-fry for 1–2 minutes, and when the dhal turns light brown, add the curry leaves. Fry, stirring constantly, for 2 minutes.

Pour the spiced oil over the cabbage, stir in the coconut, season with salt and black pepper, and serve hot.

For mild-spiced cabbage bhaji, heat a small saucepan, then add 1–2 tablespoons vegetable oil. When hot, add 1 tablespoon cumin seeds, 2 garlic cloves, thinly sliced, and 1 teaspoon chopped ginger. Stir-fry for 1–2 minutes, then pour the oil over the prepared cabbage, as above. Season and serve hot. **Calories per serving 112**

spicy fish

Calories per serving **113**
Serves **2**
Preparation time **10 minutes,**
  plus marinating
Cooking time **5 minutes**

1 **garlic clove**, peeled
2 **red shallots**, chopped
1 **lemon grass stalk**
½ teaspoon **ground turmeric**
½ teaspoon **ground ginger**
1 **mild fresh red chile,** seeded
  and coarsely chopped
1 tablespoon **peanut oil**
2 teaspoon **fish sauce**
10 oz **boneless white**
  fish fillets, cut into
  bite-size pieces
salt and **black pepper**
1 tablespoon chopped **fresh**
  cilantro, to garnish

Put the garlic, shallots, lemon grass, turmeric, ginger, chile, and salt and black pepper into a food processor or blender and process until a paste is formed, adding the oil and fish sauce to help the grinding.

Place the fish in a bowl and toss with the spice paste. Cover and refrigerate for 15 minutes.

Thread the pieces of fish onto skewers and arrange on an aluminum foil-lined pan. Cook under a preheated hot broiler for 4–5 minutes, turning once so that the pieces brown evenly. Serve sprinkled with the cilantro.

For Chinese greens to serve as an accompaniment, put 3 cups raw shredded Chinese greens in a saucepan of boiling water and cook for 1–2 minutes. Drain and place on warmed serving plates. Heat 1 teaspoon peanut oil in a small saucepan and cook ½ teaspoon finely chopped garlic briefly. Stir in 1 teaspoon oyster sauce, 1 tablespoon water, and ½ tablespoon sesame oil, then bring to a boil. Pour the mxiture over the greens and toss together. **Calories per serving 35**

trivandrum beet curry

Calories per serving **122**
Serves **4**
Preparation time **15 minutes**
Cooking time **25–30 minutes**

1 tablespoon **peanut oil**
1 teaspoon **black mustard
  seeds**
1 **onion**, chopped
2 **garlic cloves**, chopped
2 **fresh red chiles**, seeded
  and finely chopped
8 **curry leaves**
1 teaspoon **ground turmeric**
1 teaspoon **cumin seeds**
1 **cinnamon stick**
5 **raw beets**, peeled and cut
  into matchsticks
1 cup canned **diced tomatoes**
1 cup **water**
scant ½ cup **reduced-fat
  coconut milk**
juice of 1 **lime**
salt
chopped **fresh cilantro
  leaves**, to garnish

Heat the oil in a wok or saucepan over medium heat. Add the mustard seeds and as soon as they begin to "pop" (after a few seconds), add the onion, garlic, and chiles. Cook for about 5 minutes, until the onion is soft and translucent.

Add the remaining spices and the beets. Cook for another 1–2 minutes, then add the tomatoes, measured water, and a pinch of salt. Simmer for 15–20 minutes, stirring occasionally, until the beets are tender.

Stir in the coconut milk and simmer for another 1–2 minutes, until the sauce has thickened. Stir in the lime juice and check the seasoning. Garnish with chopped cilantro and serve immediately.

For spiced beet salad, thickly slice 12 cooked beets (about 1¼ lb) and arrange on a wide serving plate with 1 thinly sliced red onion and a large handful of arugula leaves. Make a dressing by whisking 1 cup reduced-fat coconut milk with 1 tablespoon curry powder and ¼ cup each of very finely chopped cilantro and mint. Season to taste and drizzle it over the beet salad. Toss to mix well and serve. **Calories per serving 120**

coconut, carrot, & spinach salad

Calories per serving **129**
Serves **4**
Preparation time **10 minutes**
Cooking time **1 minute**

2 (5 oz) packages **baby spinach,** finely chopped
1 **carrot**, coarsely grated
⅓ cup grated **fresh coconut** or **unsweetened dried coconut**
2 tablespoons **peanut oil**
2 teaspoons **black mustard seeds**
1 teaspoon **cumin seeds**
juice of 1 **lime**
juice of 1 **orange**
salt and **black pepper**

Place the spinach in a large bowl with the carrot and coconut, and toss together lightly.

Heat the oil a small skillet over medium heat. Add the mustard and cumin seeds, and stir-fry for 20–30 seconds, until fragrant and the mustard seeds start to "pop."

Remove from the heat and pour the mxiture over the salad with the lime and orange juice. Season well and toss before serving.

For spicy coconut, carrot & spinach sauté, heat 1 tablespoon peanut oil in a large wok or skillet and add 1 finely diced red chile, 2 finely chopped garlic cloves, 4 finely sliced scallions, and 1 teaspoon each of cumin and black mustard seeds. Stir-fry for 1 minute, then add 1 shredded carrot. Stir-fry for 2–3 minutes and add 7 cups) baby spinach. Stir-fry over high heat for 2–3 minutes or until the spinach has just wilted. Season, sprinkle with ⅓ cup grated fresh coconut or unsweetend dried coconut and serve immediately.
Calories per serving 90

carrot & red cabbage slaw

Calories per serving **137**
Serves **4**
Preparation time **10 minutes**
Cooking time **1 minute**

3 large **carrots,** coarsely
    grated
3 cups finely shredded
    red cabbage
juice of 2 **limes**
2 teaspoons **agave syrup**
2 tablespoons **light olive oil**
1 **fresh red chile,** finely diced
1 tablespoon **black mustard
    seeds**
salt and **black pepper**

Place the carrots and red cabbage in a large bowl. Mix together the lime juice and agave syrup, and stir into the vegetables. Toss to mix well, and set aside.

Heat the oil in a small skillet over medium heat. Add the chile and mustard seeds, and stir-fry for 20–30 seconds, until fragrant and the mustard seeds start to "pop."

Scrape the contents of the skillet over the salad, season well, and toss to combine. Serve immediately.

For toasted spiced chapati wedges to serve as an accompaniment, cut 4 prepared chapatis or other flatbreads into wedges and arrange on 2 large baking sheets. Lightly spray with cooking oil spray and sprinkle with 1 tablespoon crushed cumin seeds, 1 tablespoon nigella seeds, 2 teaspoons mild chili powder, and a little sea salt. Cook in a preheated oven, at 350°F, for 8–10 minutes or until crisp. Serve hot. **Calories per serving 255**

cucumber lassi

Calories per serving **140**
Makes 1⅔ **cups**

½ **cucumber**
⅔ cup **plain yogurt**
½ cup ice-cold **water**
handful of **mint**
½ teaspoon **ground cumin**
squeeze of **lemon juice**

Peel and coarsely chop the cucumber. Place in a food processor or blender and add the yogurt and iced water.

Pull the mint leaves off their stems, reserving a few for decoration. Chop the remainder coarsely and put them into the food processor. Add the cumin and lemon juice and process briefly.

Pour the smoothie into a tall glass, decorate with mint leaves, if desired, and serve immediately.

For mango lassi, cut the flesh of a mango into cubes and add it to a food processor or blender with ⅔ cup plain yogurt and the same amount of ice-cold water, 1 tablespoon rose water, and ¼ teaspoon ground cardamom. Process briefly and serve. **Calories per serving 276**

peanut & cucumber salad

Calories per serving **147**
Serves **4**
Preparation time **5 minutes**
Cooking time **5 minutes**

1 large **cucumber**, peeled and
   finely chopped
¼ cup **lemon juice**
1 tablespoon **light olive oil**
1 teaspoon **yellow mustard
   seeds**
2 teaspoons **black mustard
   seeds**
8–10 **curry leaves**
1–2 **fresh red chiles**, seeded
   and finely chopped
¼ cup finely chopped **roasted
   peanuts**
salt and **pepper**

Place the cucumber in a large bowl, sprinkle with the lemon juice, and season with salt. Stir to mix well and set aside.

Heat the oil in a small skillet over medium heat. Add the mustard seeds, curry leaves, and chile, and stir-fry for 1–2 minutes, until fragrant and the mustard seeds start to "pop."

Add the contents of the pan to the cucumber mixture. Toss to mix well, sprinkle with the chopped peanuts, and serve immediately.

For spicy roasted tomato salad, cut 10 medium plum or roma tomatoes in half and place on a baking sheet, cut side up. Season and sprinkle with 1 tablespoon mild curry powder and 2 teaspoons cumin seeds. Lightly spray with cooking oil spray and roast in a preheated oven, at 400°F, for 12–15 minutes. Let cool. Arrange 7 cups mixed salad greens on a wide serving plate with ½ sliced red onion. Arrange the cooled tomatoes over the salad, squeeze the juice of 2 limes over the top, and sprinkle with ¼ cup toasted pumpkin seeds. **Calories per serving 133**

green masala chicken kebabs

Calories per serving **148**
Serves **4**
Preparation time **10 minutes,
  plus marinating**
Cooking time **10 minutes**

4 boneless, skinless **chicken
  breasts**, cubed
juice of 1 **lime**
½ cup **fat-free plain yogurt**
1 teaspoon peeled and finely
  grated **fresh ginger root**
1 **garlic clove**, crushed
1 **fresh green chile,** seeded
  and chopped
large handful of finely chopped
  fresh cilantro leaves
large handful of finely chopped
  mint leaves
1 tablespoon **medium curry
  powder**
pinch of **salt**
lime wedges, to serve

Put the chicken into a large bowl. Put all the remaining ingredients into a food processor and blend until smooth, adding a little water, if necessary. Pour the marinade over the chicken, and toss to mix well. Cover and let marinate in the refrigerator overnight.

Preheat the broiler until hot. Thread the chicken onto 8 metal skewers and broil for 6–8 minutes, turning once or twice, until the chicken is cooked through. Serve immediately with lime wedges for squeezing.

For red masala chicken kebabs, mix ¼ cup fat-free plain yogurt with ¼ cup tomato paste, 1 teaspoon grated ginger, 4 crushed garlic cloves, 1 tablespoon chili powder, 1 teaspoon ground cumin, and 1 teaspoon turmeric. Pour the mixture over the chicken and marinate and cook as above. **Calories per serving 152**

dry shrimp curry

Calories per serving **157**
Serves **4**
Preparation time **10 minutes**
Cooking time **10 minutes**

1 **onion**, coarsely chopped
4 **garlic cloves**, chopped
½ cup **lemon juice**
1 teaspoon peeled and finely
  grated **fresh ginger root**
1 teaspoon **ground turmeric**
½ teaspoon **chili powder**
2 teaspoons store-bought
  medium curry paste
1 tablespoon **peanut oil**
1 lb **raw jumbo shrimp**,
  peeled and deveined
¼ cup chopped **fresh cilantro
  leaves**
4 **scallions**, finely sliced
salt

Put the onion, garlic, lemon juice, ginger, turmeric, chili powder, and curry paste into a food processor and blend until fairly smooth. Season with salt.

Heat the oil in a wide saucepan over medium heat. Add the onion paste and stir-fry for 2–3 minutes. Add the shrimp and stir-fry for another 4–5 minutes, until they turn pink and are cooked through.

Remove from the heat and stir in the cilantro and scallions. Serve immediately.

For lemon & herbed couscous, to serve as an accompaniment, put 1 ½ cups couscous into a shallow, heatproof bowl. Add enough boiling water to just cover the couscous, cover tightly, and let stand for 12–15 minutes. Fluff up the grains of the couscous with a fork, season, and stir in a large handful each of chopped cilantro and mint. Squeeze the juice of 1 lemon over the top and serve immediately. **Calories per serving 260**

tamarind & date chutney

Calories per serving **161**
Serves **4**
Preparation time **10 minutes**

1 ⅓ cups coarsely chopped
  pitted dried dates
1 tablespoon **tamarind paste**
1 teaspoon **ground cumin**
1 teaspoon **chili powder**
1 tablespoon **ketchup**
1 cup **water**
salt

Put all the ingredients into a food processor or blender and process until fairly smooth.

Transfer the mixture to a serving bowl, cover, and chill until required. The chutney will keep for up to 3 days in the refrigerator.

For chutney-marinated paneer, spoon the chutney over 8 oz paneer, cubed, and let marinate for several hours. Drain well. Cover the broiler rack with aluminum foil and brush with oil. Spread out the paneer on the foil and cook under a preheated hot broiler until browned, turning as necessary. **Calories per serving 368**

spiced beets

Calories per serving **182**
Serves **4**
Preparation time **10 minutes**
Cooking time **5–6 minutes**

1 tablespoon **vegetable oil**
2 **garlic cloves**, finely chopped
1 teaspoon grated **fresh ginger root**
1 teaspoon **cumin seeds**
1 teaspoon **coriander seeds**, crushed
½ teaspoon **dried red pepper flakes**
12 freshly cooked **beets** (about 1¼ lb), peeled and cut into wedges
⅔ cup **coconut milk**
¼ teaspoon **ground cardamom seeds**
grated zest and juice of 1 **lime**
handful of chopped **fresh cilantro**
salt and **black pepper**

Heat the oil in a large skillet and add the garlic, ginger, cumin seeds, coriander seeds, and red pepper flakes. Stir-fry for 1–2 minutes, then add the beets. Cook, stirring gently, for 1 minute, then add the coconut milk, cardamom, and lime zest and juice. Cook over medium heat for 2–3 minutes.

Stir in the fresh cilantro, season with salt and black pepper, and serve hot, warm, or at room temperature.

For spiced mixed vegetables, replace the beets with 8 oz cooked baby carrots (or chunks of 4 regular carrots), 2 cups cooked rutabaga cubes, and 2 thickly sliced, cooked parsnips. **Calories per serving 174**

coconut & cilantro mussels

Calories per serving **185**
Serves **4**
Preparation time **10 minutes**
Cooking time **15 minutes**

1 tablespoon **vegetable oil**
4 **scallions**, finely chopped
1 inch length **galangal** or **fresh ginger root**, shredded
1 **fresh green chile,** finely chopped
1 cup **reduced-fat coconut milk**
large bunch of **fresh cilantro**, chopped, plus extra to garnish
1 tablespoon chopped **Thai basil** (optional)
1 cup **fish stock** or **broth**
2 tablespoons **Thai fish sauce**
2 tablespoons **lime juice**
1 tablespoon **soy sauce**
1 tablespoon packed **light brown sugar**
3–4 **lime leaves**, shredded (optional)
2 lb **mussels**, scrubbed and debearded
unsweetened dried coconut, toasted, to garnish (optional)

Heat the oil in a large saucepan and cook the scallions, galangal or ginger, and chile for 2 minutes, until soft. Add the remaining ingredients except the mussels and warm gently until the sugar has dissolved. Turn up the heat and bring to boiling point, then reduce the heat and simmer gently for 5 minutes to let the flavors develop.

Transfer the mussels to the coconut sauce and cover with a tight-fitting lid. Cook for 3–4 minutes or until the mussels have opened; discard any that have not.

Spoon into serving bowls with plenty of the juices and sprinkle with extra cilantro leaves and dried coconut, if using. Serve immediately.

For coconut & cilantro seafood with lime rice, replace the mussels with 1 lb fresh or frozen prepared seafood mix and cook as above, but omitting the lime leaves. Cook 1 cup rice with the grated zest of 1 lime. Serve the rice in bowls and ladle over the seafood.
Calories per serving 484

warm cabbage salad

Calories per serving **188**
Serves **4**
Preparation time **10 minutes**
Cooking time **5–7 minutes**

2 tablespoons **sunflower oil**
2 teaspoons **black mustard seeds**
1 tablespoon finely grated **fresh ginger root**
10–12 **curry leaves**
1 small **green cabbage**, halved, cored, and finely shredded
2–3 tablespoons **grated fresh coconut** or **unsweetened dried coconut**
salt and **black pepper**
2 tablespoons **chopped roasted peanuts**, to garnish

Heat the oil in a large skillet or wok and add the mustard seeds. When they start to "pop," add the ginger, curry leaves, and cabbage and stir-fry over high heat for 4–5 minutes.

Add the grated coconut and stir-fry for another 1–2 minutes. Season well, garnish with the roasted peanuts, and serve immediately.

For sweet fennel & cabbage salad, use ½ small green cabbage, halved, cored, and finely shredded, 1 head fennel, finely shredded, and 1 large carrot, peeled and shredded. Add these to the pan with the ginger and curry leaves. Proceed as above. **Calories per serving 192**

okra, pea, & tomato curry

Calories per serving **188**
Serves **4**
Preparation time **5 minutes**
Cooking time **about
 20 minutes**

1 tablespoon **peanut oil**
6–8 **curry leaves**
2 teaspoons **black mustard
 seeds**
1 **onion**, finely diced
2 teaspoons **ground cumin**
1 teaspoon **ground coriander**
2 teaspoons **curry powder**
1 teaspoon **ground turmeric**
3 **garlic cloves**, finely chopped
1 lb **okra**, cut on the diagonal
 into 1 inch pieces
1⅓ cups **fresh** or **frozen peas**
2 ripe **plum** or **roma
 tomatoes**, finely chopped
salt and **black pepper**
3 tablespoons **grated fresh
 coconut** or **unsweetened
 dried**, to serve

Heat the oil in a large, nonstick wok or skillet over medium heat. Add the curry leaves, mustard seeds, and onion. Stir-fry for 3–4 minutes, until fragrant and the onion is starting to soften, then add the cumin, coriander, curry powder, and turmeric. Stir-fry for another 1–2 minutes, until fragrant.

Add the garlic and okra, and increase the heat to high. Cook, stirring, for 2–3 minutes, then add the peas and tomatoes. Season to taste, cover, and reduce the heat to low. Cook gently for 10–12 minutes, stirring occasionally, until the okra is just tender. Remove from the heat and sprinkle with the grated coconut just before serving.

For spiced seeded pea & tomato pilaf, put 1½ cups basmati rice into a medium saucepan with 2 teaspoons dry-roasted cumin seeds, 1 tablespoon crushed dry-roasted coriander seeds, 2 teaspoons black mustard seeds, 1⅓ cups fresh or frozen peas and 3 peeled, seeded, and finely chopped tomatoes. Add 3⅔ cups boiling vegetable stock or broth, bring to a boil, and season to taste. Reduce the heat to low, cover the pan, and cook gently for 10–12 minutes or until all the liquid has been absorbed. Remove from the heat and let stand, covered and undisturbed, for 10–15 minutes. Fluff up the grains with a fork and serve. **Calories per serving 343**

cauliflower & chickpea curry

Calories per serving **194**
  (not including mint raita)
Serves **4**
Preparation time **10 minutes**
Cooking time **about 20 minutes**

1 tablespoon **peanut oil**
8 **scallions,** cut into 2 inch
  lengths
2 teaspoons grated **garlic**
2 teaspoons **ground ginger**
2 tablespoons **medium curry**
  powder
2 cups **cauliflower florets**
1 **red bell pepper**, cored,
  seeded, and diced
1 **yellow bell pepper**, cored,
  seeded, and diced
1⅔ cups canned **diced**
  tomatoes
1⅔ cups rinsed and drained,
  canned **chickpeas**
salt and **black pepper**

Heat the oil in a large, nonstick skillet over medium heat. Add the scallions and stir-fry for 2–3 minutes. Add the garlic, ginger, and curry powder, and stir-fry for 20–30 seconds, until fragrant. Now add the cauliflower and bell peppers, and stir-fry for another 2–3 minutes.

Stir in the tomatoes and bring to a boil. Cover, reduce the heat to medium, and simmer for 10 minutes, stirring occasionally. Add the chickpeas, season to taste, and bring back to a boil. Remove from the heat and serve immediately with mint raita, if desired.

For broccoli & black-eyed pea curry, follow the recipe above replacing the cauliflower with 4 cups broccoli florets and the chickpeas with 2½ cups rinsed and drained black-eyed peas. **Calories per serving 193**

mulligatawny soup

Calories per serving **197**
Serves **4**
Preparation time **15 minutes**
Cooking time **50 minutes**

4 tablespoons **butter**
1 large **onion**, thinly sliced
1 small **carrot**, cut into small
  dice
1 large **celery stick**, finely
  chopped
3 tablespoons **flour**
2 teaspoons **curry powder**
3¾ cups **vegetable stock**
  or **broth**
1 large **Granny Smith** or
  other cooking apple
2 teaspoons **lemon juice**
2 tablespoons cooked
  basmati rice or **other**
  long grain rice
fresh **flat leaf parsley leaves**,
  coarsely chopped, to garnish

Melt the butter in a saucepan and gently sauté the onion, carrot, and celery until soft. Do not let them brown. Stir in the flour and curry powder. Cook for 2 minutes and pour in the stock or broth.

Bring to a boil, stirring constantly. Reduce the heat, cover with a lid, and simmer gently for 30 minutes, stirring occasionally.

Peel, core, and dice the apple, then add to the soup with the lemon juice and rice. Season to taste and simmer for another 10 minutes. Serve hot garnished with a sprinkling of parsley.

For lamb mulligatawny, cut 1 lb boneless shoulder or leg of lamb into bite-size pieces. Lightly brown the meat for 3–5 minutes before adding the onion, carrot, and celery. Proceed as above, but increase the cooking time to 45 minutes or longer, until the lamb is tender, before adding the apples. **Calories per serving 344**

recipes under 300 calories

south indian vegetable stew

Calories per serving **200**
Serves **4**
Preparation time **15 minutes**
Cooking time **20–25 minutes**

1 tablespoon **peanut oil**
6 **shallots**, halved and thinly
  sliced
2 teaspoons **black mustard
  seeds**
8–10 **curry leaves**
1 **fresh green chile,** thinly
  sliced
2 teaspoons peeled and finely
  grated **fresh ginger root**
1 teaspoon **ground turmeric**
2 teaspoons **ground cumin**
6 **black peppercorns**
2 **carrots,** cut into thick batons
1 **zucchini**, cut into thick
  batons
2 cups **green beans**, trimmed
1 **potato**, peeled and cut into
  thin batons
1⅔ cups **reduced-fat
  coconut milk**
1⅔ cups **vegetable stock**
  or **broth**
2 tablespoons **lemon juice**
salt and **black pepper**

Heat the oil in a large skillet over medium heat. Add
the shallots and stir-fry for 4–5 minutes. Add the
mustard seeds, curry leaves, chile, ginger, turmeric,
cumin, and peppercorns, and stir-fry for another
1–2 minutes, until fragrant.

Add the carrots, zucchini, beans, and potato to the pan.
Pour in the coconut milk and stock or broth and bring to
a boil. Reduce the heat to low, cover, and simmer gently
for 12–15 minutes, until the vegetables are tender.
Season to taste, remove from the heat, and squeeze the
lemon juice over the top just before serving.

For spicy tomato, vegetable & coconut curry, follow
the recipe above, replacing the turmeric, cumin, and
black peppercorns with 2 tablespoons hot curry powder,
and the vegetable stock with 1⅔ cups tomato puree or
tomato sauce. **Calories per serving 231**

whole pomfret in banana leaf

Calories per serving **206**
Serves **4**
Preparation time **20 minutes**
Cooking time **15–20 minutes**

1 large **pomfret**, **grouper**, or
Chilean sea bass, gutted
and cleaned
1 **banana leaf**, large enough
to wrap the fish in
2 inch piece of **fresh ginger
root**, peeled and cut into
matchsticks
¼ cup **coconut cream**
⅓ cup chopped **fresh cilantro**
⅓ cup chopped **mint**
⅓ cup **lime juice**
3 **scallions**, finely sliced
4 **lime leaves**, finely shredded
2 **fresh red chiles**, seeded
and finely sliced
salt and **black pepper**

Use a small sharp knife to score the fish flesh
diagonally on both sides. Dip the banana leaf into
boiling water for 15–20 seconds to make it supple and
pliable for wrapping the fish. Remove and rinse under
cold water. Dry with paper towels.

Mix together the ginger, coconut cream, chopped herbs,
lime juice, scallions, lime leaves, and chile in a bowl.
Season the mixture to taste.

Lay the banana leaf on a work surface and place the
fish in the center. Spread the herb mixture over the fish
and wrap in the leaf to form a neat package. Secure
with bamboo skewers or toothpicks.

Place the package in a large bamboo steamer and
steam, covered, over a wok or large saucepan of
simmering water for 15–20 minutes or until the fish
is cooked through.

For stuffed spicy trout, divide the herb mix among
4 cleaned trout, placing it in the body cavities. Marinate
for 30 minutes, then bake in an ovenproof dish, at
375°F, for about 30 minutes, until cooked and aromatic.
Calories per serving 256

green curry with straw mushrooms

Calories per serving **225**
Serves **4**
Preparation time **10 minutes**
Cooking time **10 minutes**

1 ¼ cups **coconut milk**, plus
   extra for drizzling
2 ½ tablespoons **green curry
   paste**
1 ¼ cups **vegetable stock
   or broth**
2 **eggplants**, coarsely
   chopped into large chunks
3 tablespoons packed **light
   brown sugar**
4 teaspoons **soy sauce**
¼ cup peeled and finely
   chopped **fresh ginger root**
2 cups drained, canned **straw
   mushrooms**,
½ **green bell pepper**, cored,
   seeded, and thinly sliced
salt

Put most of the coconut milk and the curry paste into a saucepan over medium heat and stir well. Pour in the stock or broth, then add the eggplants, sugar, soy sauce, ginger, and salt to taste.

Bring to a boil and cook, stirring, for 5 minutes. Add the mushrooms and green bell pepper, reduce the heat, and cook for 2 minutes, until piping hot.

Serve in bowls, drizzled with a little extra coconut milk.

For vegetable korma, heat 1 tablespoon vegetable oil in a large saucepan, add 1 finely diced onion, 3 bruised cardamom pods, 2 teaspoons each of ground cumin and ground coriander, and ½ teaspoon turmeric, and cook over low heat for 5–6 minutes or until the onion is light golden brown. Add 1 seeded and chopped green chile, 1 crushed garlic clove, and a thumb-size piece of fresh ginger root, peeled and grated, and cook for 1 minute, then add about 3 cups of prepared mixed vegetables, such as cauliflower, bell peppers, carrots, and zucchini,, and cook for another 5 minutes. Remove the pan from the heat and stir through 1 cup yogurt and 2 tablespoons ground almonds. Serve sprinkled with chopped cilantro. **Calories per serving 181**

monkfish kebabs

Calories per serving **211**
Serves **4**
Preparation time **10 minutes,
plus marinating**
Cooking time **8–10 minutes**

2 lb **monkfish fillet**, cut into
  1½ inch cubes
1 cup **plain yogurt**
¼ cup **lemon juice**
3 **garlic cloves**, crushed
2 teaspoons grated **fresh
  ginger root**
1 teaspoon **hot chili powder**
1 teaspoon **ground cumin**
1 teaspoon **ground coriander**
2 **fresh red chiles**, finely
  sliced
salt and **black pepper**

To garnish
chopped **fresh cilantro**
lime slices
sliced **fresh red chiles**

Put the monkfish cubes into a nonmetallic bowl.

Mix together the yogurt, lemon juice, garlic, ginger, chili powder, cumin, ground coriander, and chiles in a small bowl, and season with salt and black pepper. Pour the mixture over the fish, cover, and marinate in the refrigerator overnight, if time permits.

Lift the fish out of the marinade and thread onto 8 flat metal skewers. Place on a broiler rack and cook under a preheated hot broiler for 8–10 minutes, turning once, until the fish is cooked through. Serve hot, garnished with chopped fresh cilantro, lime slices, and chile slices.

For tandoori whiting fillets, make a marinade using 1 cup plain yogurt, ¼ cup lemon juice, 2 garlic cloves, crushed, 1 teaspoon grated fresh ginger root, and 1 teaspoon ground coriander. Place 4 (7 oz) whiting fillets in a nonmetallic dish and pour over the marinade. Marinate the fish in the tandoori mixture overnight and cook as above. **Calories per serving 197**

spicy zucchini fritters

Calories per serving **211**
Serves **4**
Preparation time **15 minutes,
plus draining**
Cooking time **10–15 minutes**

3 **zucchini**
2 large **scallions**, grated
1 **garlic clove**, finely chopped
finely grated zest of 1 **lemon**
¼ cup **chickpea (besan) flour**
2 teaspoons **medium curry
powder**
1 **fresh red chile,** seeded and
finely chopped
2 tablespoons finely chopped
mint leaves
2 tablespoons finely chopped
fresh cilantro leaves
2 **eggs**, lightly beaten
2 tablespoons **light olive oil**
salt and **black pepper**

Grate the zucchini into a colander. Sprinkle lightly with salt and let drain for at least 1 hour. Squeeze out the remaining liquid.

Put the remaining ingredients, except the eggs and olive oil, into a mixing bowl and add the zucchini. Season lightly, keeping in mind you have already salted the zucchini, and mix well. Add the eggs and mix again to combine.

Heat half the olive oil in a large skillet over medium-high heat. Place tablespoonfuls of the mixture, well spaced, in the pan and press down with the back of the spoon. Cook for 1–2 minutes on each side, until golden brown and cooked through. Remove from the pan and keep warm. Repeat to cook the rest of the fritters in the same way, adding the remaining oil to the pan when necessary.

For cucumber, mango & fromage blanc relish, to serve as an accompaniment, peel, seed, and coarsely grate 1 cucumber into a fine mesh strainer. Squeeze out any excess liquid using the back of a spoon. Place the grated cucumber in a bowl with 2 tablespoons hot mango chutney and 1 cup fat-free fromage frais or Greek-style yogurt. Stir in a small handful of finely chopped cilantro leaves, season, and chill until required.
Calories per serving 60

souffléd curried omelet

Calories per serving **212**
Serves **4**
Preparation time **25 minutes**
Cooking time **about
  20 minutes**

1 tablespoon **peanut oil**
4 **garlic cloves**, crushed
8 **scallions**, finely sliced
1 **fresh red chile,** finely sliced
1 tablespoon **medium curry
  powder**
4 **tomatoes**, peeled, seeded,
  and finely chopped
small handful of finely chopped
  fresh cilantro leaves
small handful of finely chopped
  mint leaves
8 extra-large **eggs**, separated
salt and **black pepper**

Heat half the oil in an ovenproof skillet over medium heat. Add the garlic, scallions, and red chile and stir-fry for 1–2 minutes. Stir in the curry powder, tomatoes, and chopped herbs and stir-fry for 20–30 seconds. Remove from the heat, season to taste, and let cool slightly.

Place the egg whites in a large bowl and whisk until soft peaks form. Gently beat the egg yolks in a separate bowl, then fold into the egg whites with the tomato mixture until well combined.

Wipe out the pan with paper towels and place over a medium heat. Add the remaining oil and, when hot, pour in the egg mixture. Reduce the heat and cook gently for 8–10 minutes or until the bottom is starting to set. Transfer the pan to a preheated medium-hot broiler and cook for 4–5 minutes or until the top is puffed, lightly golden, and almost set. Serve immediately with a crisp green salad.

For Indian spicy scrambled eggs, heat 1 tablespoon peanut oil in a large nonstick skillet over gentle heat. Beat 8 eggs in a bowl and add 1 finely chopped red onion, 2 sliced green chiles, 1 finely chopped tomato, 1 teaspoon grated peeled ginger, and a small handful of finely chopped cilantro leaves. Season, pour into the pan, and cook, stirring occasionally, for 5–6 minutes or until lightly scrambled. **Calories per serving 200**

crab malabar-hill

Calories per serving **214**
Serves **4**
Preparation time **10 minutes**
Cooking time **5–6 minutes**

2 tablespoons **vegetable oil**
3 **garlic cloves**, finely chopped
2 teaspoons finely chopped
  fresh ginger root
6 **scallions**, very thinly sliced
3 **fresh red chiles**, seeded
  and finely sliced
1 1/4 lb **fresh white crab meat**
grated zest and juice of **1 lime**
1/4 cup chopped **fresh cilantro**
2 tablespoons chopped **mint**
  leaves
salt and **black pepper**
crisp **lettuce leaves**, to serve

Heat the oil in a large wok or nonstick skillet and add the garlic, ginger, scallions, and chiles. Sauté, stirring constantly, for 2–3 minutes.

Add the crab meat, lime zest and juice, cilantro, and mint. Stir-fry for 2–3 minutes, season with salt and black pepper, and serve hot on top of crisp lettuce leaves.

For spicy crab omelets, use this spicy, tangy crab mixture as the filling. Make 4 thin omelets, using 2 eggs each, in a nonstick skillet. Divide the crab mixture among them and fold over to enclose it. Serve with a crisp green salad. **Calories per serving 329**

thai red pork & bean curry

Calories per serving **216**
Serves **4**
Preparation time **10 minutes**
Cooking time **5 minutes**

2 tablespoons **peanut oil**
1½ tablespoons **Thai red curry paste**
12 oz **lean pork**, sliced into thin strips
1 cup halved **green beans**
2 tablespoons **Thai fish sauce**
1 teaspoon **sugar**
Chinese chives or **regular chives**, to garnish

Heat the oil in a wok or large skillet over medium heat until the oil starts to shimmer, add the curry paste, and cook, stirring, until it releases its aroma.

Add the pork and beans and stir-fry for 2–3 minutes or until the meat is cooked through and the beans are just tender.

Stir in the fish sauce and sugar and serve, garnished with Chinese chives or regular chives.

For chicken green curry with sugar snap peas, replace the red curry paste with 1½ tablespoons green curry paste, the pork with 12 oz sliced chicken breast, and the green beans with 1 cup sliced sugar snap peas. Cook as above, adding a dash of lime juice before serving. **Calories per serving 204**

sri lankan scallop curry

Calories per serving **216**
Serves **4**
Preparation time **10 minutes**
Cooking time **20–25 minutes**

1 tablespoon **peanut oil**
¼ teaspoon **turmeric**
1 teaspoon **cumin seeds**
2 **fresh red chiles**, seeded
  and chopped
1 **onion**, finely chopped
6 **tomatoes**, peeled, seeded,
  and diced
3 tablespoons **medium curry**
  powder
1 tablespoon **coconut cream**
1 teaspoon **ground cumin**
1 teaspoon **garam masala**
13 oz **fresh sea scallops**
small handful of finely chopped
  fresh cilantro leaves
salt and **pepper**

Heat the oil in a skillet over low heat. Add the turmeric, cumin seeds, and chiles, and sauté briefly to release the flavors. Add the onion and cook gently for 10 minutes, until softened but not browned.

Stir in the tomatoes and curry powder and simmer for 5 minutes or until the tomatoes have cooked down to a thick sauce. Stir in the coconut cream, ground cumin, and garam masala and season to taste.

Add the scallops and cook for a few minutes, until the scallops are just cooked through. Check the seasoning and adjust, if necessary. Stir in the cilantro and serve immediately.

For homemade garam masala, put ¼ cup coriander seeds, 2 tablespoons cumin seeds, 1 tablespoon black peppercorns, 1 tablespoon ground ginger, 1 teaspoon cardamom seeds, 4 cloves, 1 cinnamon stick, and 1 crushed dried bay leaf into a skillet. Dry-roast over medium-low heat for a few minutes, until fragrant. Remove from the heat and let cool. Transfer the contents of the pan to a mini blender or clean electric coffee grinder, and grind to a fine powder. Store in an airtight container for up to 1 month, or in the refrigerator for up to 3 months. **Calories per tablespoon 2**

thai mussel curry with ginger

Calories per serving **217**
Serves **4**
Preparation time **30 minutes**
Cooking time **15 minutes**

½–1 **fresh red chile**

2 **shallots**, quartered

1 **lemon grass stalk**

1 tablespoon peeled and finely chopped **fresh ginger root**

1 tablespoon **peanut oil**

1⅔ cups **reduced-fat coconut milk**

4–5 **kaffir lime leaves**

⅔ cup **fish stock** or **broth**

2 teaspoons **Thai fish sauce**

3 lb **mussels**, scrubbed and debearded

small bunch of **fresh cilantro**, torn into pieces, to garnish

Put the chile, shallots, lemon grass, and ginger into a mini blender and blend until finely chopped.

Heat the oil in large, deep saucepan, add the finely chopped ingredients, and sauté over medium heat for 5 minutes, stirring until softened. Add the coconut milk, lime leaves, fish stock or broth, and fish sauce and cook for 3 minutes.

Add the mussels, cover the pan, and cook for about 5 minutes or until the mussel shells have opened, discarding any that do not open. Spoon into warm bowls and serve garnished with cilantro.

For Thai chicken & eggplant curry, prepare the above recipe up to the end of the second step, replacing the fish stock with 1 cup chicken stock or broth. Stir in 1 diced eggplant and 10 oz boneless, skinless chicken breast, cut into large chunks. Bring back to a boil, cover, and simmer for 12–15 minutes, or until the chicken is cooked and the eggplant tender. Serve sprinkled with cilantro. **Calories per serving 218**

singapore curried scallops

Calories per serving **225**
Serves **4**
Preparation time **10 minutes**
Cooking time **5 minutes**

24 fresh **sea scallops**
3 tablespoons **mild curry powder**
1 tablespoon **peanut oil**
¼ cup **light soy sauce**
2 tablespoons **rice wine**
2 **fresh red chiles**, finely sliced
3 inch piece of **fresh ginger root**, peeled and finely shredded
6 **scallions**, finely sliced
salt and **black pepper**

Put the scallops onto a plate, dust the curry powder over them, and lightly season to taste. Toss to mix well.

Heat the oil in a large, nonstick skillet. When hot, add the scallops, spacing them out around the pan. Sear for 1–2 minutes on each side, then remove from the pan and arrange on a warm serving plate.

Mix together the soy sauce and rice wine and sprinkle over the scallops. Sprinkle a little chile, ginger, and scallion over each one, and serve immediately.

For mild scallop & coconut curry, heat 1 tablespoon peanut oil in a large skillet and add 1 finely chopped onion, 1 seeded and finely chopped red chile, 2 finely chopped garlic cloves, and 1 teaspoon finely diced ginger. Stir-fry for 3–4 minutes or until the onion has just softened, then add 1 tablespoon mild curry powder and stir-fry for 1 minute. Add 1⅔ cups reduced-fat coconut milk and 1 cup tomato puree or tomato sauce and bring to a boil. Reduce the heat to medium and cook for 6–8 minutes, stirring often. Season to taste, stir in 24 fresh sea scallops, and cook for 4–5 minutes or until they are just cooked through. Remove from the heat and serve in warm bowls.
Calories per serving 313

indian-spiced squash wedges

Calories per serving **292**
Serves **4**
Preparation time **15 minutes**,
  plus cooling
Cooking time **15–20 minutes**

2 lb **winter squash**, such as
  acorn squash, **butternut
  squash**, or **pumpkin**
1 teaspoon **cumin seeds**
1 teaspoon **coriander seeds**
2 **cardamom pods**
3 tablespoons **sunflower oil**
1 teaspoon **sugar** or
  mango chutney

Coconut pesto
⅔ cup **fresh cilantro leaves**
1 **garlic clove**, crushed
1 **fresh green chile,** seeded
  and chopped
pinch of **sugar**
1 tablespoon **pistachio nuts**,
  coarsely chopped
⅓ cup **coconut cream**
1 tablespoon **lime juice**
salt and **black pepper**

Cut the squash into thin wedges about ½ inch
thick, discarding the seeds and fibers, and put into
a large dish.

Heat a heavy skillet until hot, add the whole spices, and
dry-fry over medium heat, stirring, until browned. Let
cool, then grind to a powder in a spice grinder or in a
mortar with a pestle. Mix the ground spices with the oil
and sugar or mango chutney in a small bowl, then add
to the squash wedges and toss well to coat.

Cook the squash wedges under a preheated hot broiler,
or over a preheated hot gas barbecue or the hot coals
of a charcoal barbecue, for 6–8 minutes on each side,
until charred and tender.

Meanwhile, make the pesto. Put the cilantro leaves,
garlic, chile, sugar, and pistachio nuts into a food
processor and process until fairly finely ground and
blended. Season with salt and black pepper. Add the
coconut cream and lime juice and process again.
Transfer to a serving bowl. Serve the wedges hot with
the coconut pesto.

For Indian-spiced sweet potato wedges, cook
4 scrubbed, large sweet potatoes (about 8 oz) each, in
a large saucepan of simmering water for 15 minutes,
or until just tender, then drain. When cool enough to
handle, slice into large wedges. Toss with the spice and
oil mixture and broil or barbecue, as above, for about
6 minutes, turning frequently, until browned. Serve hot
with the coconut pesto. **Calories per serving 419**

creamy shrimp curry

Calories per serving **248**
(not including rice)
Serves **4**
Preparation time **10 minutes**
Cooking time **about
10 minutes**

2 tablespoons **vegetable oil**
1 **onion**, halved and finely
sliced
2 **garlic cloves**, finely sliced
1 inch piece of **fresh ginger
root**, peeled and finely
chopped
1 tablespoon **ground
coriander**
1 tablespoon **ground cumin**
½ teaspoon **turmeric**
1 cup **coconut milk**
½ cup **vegetable stock**
1¼ lb frozen, large, cooked
peeled shrimp, defrosted
grated zest and juice of 1 **lime**
¼ cup finely chopped **fresh
cilantro leaves**
salt and **black pepper**

Heat the oil in a large saucepan, add the onion, garlic,
and ginger and cook for 4–5 minutes. Add the ground
coriander, cumin, and turmeric and cook, stirring, for
1 minute.

Pour in the coconut milk and stock and bring to a boil.
Reduce the heat and simmer for 2–3 minutes. Stir in
the shrimp and lime zest and juice, then simmer for
2 minutes or until the shrimp are heated through.

Stir in the chopped cilantro and season well with
salt and black pepper. Serve immediately with boiled
basmati or jasmine rice.

calcutta beef curry

Calories per serving **250**
Serves **4**
Preparation time **20 minutes,**
 plus marinating
Cooking time **1 hour**
 20 minutes

13 oz **boneless beef chuck**
 or **beef round**, cut into bite-
 size pieces
⅓ cup **plain yogurt**
1 tablespoon **medium**
 curry powder
2 tablespoons **mustard oil**
1 **dried bay leaf**
1 **cinnamon stick**
3 **cloves**
4 **green cardamom pods**,
 bruised
1 **large onion**, halved and
 thinly sliced
3 **garlic cloves**, crushed
1 teaspoon finely grated
 fresh ginger root
1 teaspoon **ground turmeric**
1 teaspoon **hot chili powder**
2 teaspoons **ground cumin**
1⅔ cups **beef stock** or **broth**
salt

Put the meat into a nonmetallic bowl. Mix together the yogurt and curry powder and pour it over the meat. Season with salt, cover, and marinate in the refrigerator for 24 hours.

Heat the oil in a large, nonstick wok or skillet and add the spices. Stir-fry for 1 minute, then add the onion. Stir-fry over medium heat for 4–5 minutes, then add the garlic, ginger, turmeric, chili powder, and cumin. Add the marinated meat and stir-fry for 10–15 minutes over low heat.

Pour in the beef stock or broth and bring to a boil. Reduce the heat to low, cover tightly, and simmer gently, stirring occasionally, for 1 hour or until the meat is tender. Check the seasoning, remove from the heat, and serve immediately.

For Calcutta chicken curry, use 4 chicken thighs and 4 chicken drumsticks instead of the beef. Also replace the beef stock with chicken stock or broth. Follow the same instructions as the recipe above. Add ¾ cup sliced dried apricots for a hint of sweetness, stirring them in with the stock. **Calories per serving 424**

eggplant thai green curry

Calories per serving **262**
Serves **4**
Preparation time **7 minutes**
Cooking time **7–10 minutes**

1¼ cups **coconut milk**
2½ tablespoons **Thai green curry paste** (see page 208)
1¼ cups **vegetable stock** or **broth**
4 **small round eggplants**, each cut into 8 pieces
2½ tablespoons **palm sugar**
1 teaspoon **salt**
4 teaspoons **vegetarian Thai fish sauce**
¾ inch piece **galangal** or **fresh ginger root**, peeled
2⅓ cups drained, canned **straw mushrooms**
½ **green bell pepper**, thinly sliced

To garnish
handful of **Thai basil leaves**
2 tablespoons **coconut milk**

Heat the coconut milk in a saucepan with the curry paste, stirring to mix well. Add the stock and then the eggplants, sugar, salt, fish sauce, galangal or ginger, and mushrooms.

Bring to a boil and cook, stirring, for 2 minutes.

Add the green bell pepper, lower the heat, and cook for 1 minute. Serve in a bowl, garnished with the basil leaves and drizzled with coconut milk. Discard the piece of galangal or ginger root before serving.

For bamboo shoot & water chestnut curry, omit the eggplants and replace with ¾ cup canned bamboo shoots and 1 cup canned sliced water chestnuts. Add at the same time as the mushrooms. Reduce the quantity of stock or broth to ⅔ cup. **Calories per serving 255**

thai squash, tofu, & pea curry

Calories per serving **264**
Serves **4**
Preparation time **15 minutes**
Cooking time **25 minutes**

1 tablespoon **peanut oil**
1 tablespoon **Thai red curry paste**
½ **butternut squash,** peeled, seeded and cubed
2 cups **vegetable stock**
1⅔ cups **reduced-fat coconut milk**
6 **kaffir lime leaves**, bruised, plus extra shredded leaves to garnish
1⅓ cups **fresh or frozen peas**
10 oz **firm tofu**, diced
2 tablespoons **light soy** sauce
juice of 1 **lime**

To garnish
fresh cilantro leaves
finely chopped **fresh red chile**

Heat the oil in a wok or deep skillet, add the curry paste, and stir-fry over low heat for 1 minute. Add the squash, stir-fry briefly, and then add the stock, coconut milk, and lime leaves.

Bring to a boil, then cover, reduce the heat, and simmer gently for 15 minutes, until the squash is tender.

Stir in the peas, tofu, soy sauce, and lime juice and simmer for another 5 minutes, until the peas are cooked. Spoon into serving bowls and garnish with shredded lime leaves, chopped cilantro, and red chile.

For Thai green vegetable curry, use green curry paste (see page 208 for homemade) instead of red curry paste. Replace the squash with 1 sliced carrot, 1 sliced zucchini, and 1 cored, seeded, and sliced red bell pepper and follow the recipe above. **Calories per serving 245**

lebanese tomato & zucchini curry

Calories per serving **266**
Serves **4**
Preparation time **5 minutes**
Cooking time **40–45 minutes**

1 tablespoon **light olive oil**
1 large **onion**, finely chopped
4 **zucchini**, cut into
  ½ × 1½ inch batons
3½ cups canned **whole plum**
  or **roma tomatoes**
2 **garlic cloves**, crushed
½ teaspoon **chili powder**
¼ teaspoon **ground turmeric**
2 teaspoons **dried mint**
salt and **black pepper**
mint leaves, to garnish
¾ cup steamed **white rice**
  per person, to serve

Heat the oil in a large saucepan over low heat. Add the onion and sauté for 10–12 minutes, until soft and translucent. Add the zucchini and cook for another 5–6 minutes, stirring occasionally.

Add the tomatoes (including the juices) and garlic, and continue to cook over medium heat for 20 minutes.

Stir in the chili powder, turmeric, and dried mint, and cook for another few minutes to let the flavors mingle. Season to taste and serve with steamed white rice.

For spicy zucchini & tomato casserole, thickly slice 4 large zucchini and arrange in the bottom of a medium ovenproof dish. Mix 1⅔ cups canned diced tomatoes with ⅓ cup tomato paste, ½ cup vegetable stock or broth, 1 tablespoon hot curry powder, 2 teaspoons each of finely grated garlic and ginger, and 2 teaspoons dried mint. Season to taste and spoon the mixture over the zucchini. Cover with aluminum foil and cook in a preheated oven, at 350°F, for 25–30 minutes. Remove from the oven and serve with steamed rice. **Calories per serving 284**

spicy chicken & mango salad

Calories per serving **279**
Serves **4**
Preparation time **15 minutes**
Cooking time **5 minutes**

4 **boneless, skinless chicken
   breasts** (about 5 oz each)
2 tablespoons **mild curry
   paste**
¼ cup **lemon juice**
⅔ cup **plain yogurt**
½ bunch of **watercress**
   or **2 cups arugula**
½ **cucumber**, diced
½ **red onion**, finely chopped
1 **mango**, peeled, pitted, and
   cut into chunks
½ **iceberg lettuce**

Cut the chicken breasts into long, thin slices. Put 4 teaspoons of the curry paste into a plastic bag with the lemon juice and mix together by squeezing the bag. Add the chicken and toss together.

Fill the bottom of a steamer halfway with water and bring to a boil. Steam the chicken in a single layer, covered, for 5 minutes, until cooked. Test with the tip of a sharp knife; the juices will run clear when it is done.

Meanwhile, mix the remaining curry paste in a bowl with the yogurt.

Tear the watercress into bite-size pieces. Add it or the arugula to the yogurt dressing with the cucumber, red onion, and mango and toss gently.

Tear the lettuce into pieces and arrange on 4 plates. Spoon the mango mixture over the top, add the warm chicken strips, and serve immediately.

For spicy shrimp, mango & avocado salad, replace the chicken with 13 oz peeled, raw jumbo shrimp with the tails on. Prepare the salad in the same way as above but add the diced flesh of an avocado. Heat 2 tablespoons vegetable or peanut oil in a nonstick skillet over high heat, and sauté 1 finely chopped red chilli for 1 minute, then add the shrimp and 2 finely chopped garlic cloves. Cook for 2 minutes, until the shrimp are pink and just cooked through. Mix through the salad and serve immediately. **Calories per serving 343**

spiced chickpeas with kale

Calories per serving **286**
Serves **4**
Preparation time **10 minutes**
Cooking time **35 minutes**

3 tablespoons **vegetable oil**
3 **red onions**, cut into wedges
2 tablespoons **mild curry paste**
1⅔ cups can **diced tomatoes**
1⅔ cups drained, canned **chickpeas**
1¼ cups **vegetable stock** or **broth**
2 teaspoons packed **light brown sugar**
1½ cups coarsely chopped **curly kale**
salt and **black pepper**

Heat the oil in a large saucepan and sauté the onions for 5 minutes, until beginning to brown. Stir in the curry paste and then the tomatoes, chickpeas, stock or broth, and sugar.

Bring to a boil, then reduce the heat, cover, and simmer gently for 20 minutes.

Stir in the kale and cook gently for another 10 minutes. Season to taste with salt and black pepper and serve.

For sesame flatbreads, to serve as an accompaniment, put 2 cups all-purpose flour, 1 teaspoon salt, and 2½ tablespoons sesame seeds into a bowl. Add 3 tablespoons vegetable oil and ½ cup cold water and mix with a blunt knife to a dough, adding a dash more water if the dough feels dry. Divide into 8 pieces and thinly roll out each piece on a lightly floured surface until about ⅛ inch thick. Heat a ridged grill pan or large dry skillet until hot and cook the flatbreads for about 2 minutes on each side, until pale golden brown. Serve one warm flatbread per person, and freeze the remainder. **Calories per serving 167**

baby eggplants with chile

Calories per serving **297**
Serves **4**
Preparation time **20 minutes**
Cooking time **25–30 minutes**

1 lb **baby eggplants**
⅓ cup **sunflower oil**
6 **garlic cloves**, finely chopped
1 tablespoon finely chopped
  fresh ginger root
8 **scallions**, cut diagonally into
  1 inch lengths
2 **fresh red chiles**, seeded
  and finely sliced
3 tablespoons **light soy sauce**
1 tablespoon **Chinese
  rice wine**
1 tablespoon **palm sugar**
small handful of **mint leaves**
small handful of coarsely
  chopped **fresh cilantro**
¾ cup coarsely chopped,
  canned **water chestnuts**
⅓ cup coarsely chopped
  roasted peanuts

Cut the eggplants in half lengthwise and put onto a heatproof plate. Place a trivet or steamer rack in a wok and pour in water to about a 2 inch depth. Bring the water to a boil and lower the eggplant plate onto the trivet or rack.

Reduce the heat, cover, and steam for 25–30 minutes (replenishing the water in the wok, if needed), until the eggplants are cooked through and soft to the touch. Remove the eggplants from the wok, transfer to a serving plate, and let cool.

Meanwhile, heat the oil in a nonstick skillet. Add the garlic, ginger, scallions, and chiles and stir-fry for 2–3 minutes. Remove from the heat and stir in the soy sauce, rice wine, and sugar.

Toss the mint leaves, cilantro, and water chestnuts with the eggplants and pour the garlic and ginger mixture evenly over the top. Sprinkle with the peanuts, toss gently, and serve immediately with lime wedges and steamed egg noodles or rice, if desired.

For eggplant with bamboo shoots, use 2 large eggplants instead of baby eggplants. Chop them into large dice and proceed as above. Add ½ cup thinly sliced, fresh red radishes and ⅔ cup drained, canned bamboo shoots instead of water chestnuts. **Calories per serving 297**

spicy crab curry

Calories per serving **299**
Serves **4**
Preparation time **15 minutes**
Cooking time **40 minutes**

2 **cooked fresh crabs**
  (about 1½ lb each)
3 **onions**, finely chopped
6 **garlic cloves**, finely chopped
1 tablespoon peeled and finely
  grated **fresh ginger root**
½ teaspoon **fenugreek seeds**
10 **curry leaves**
1 **cinnamon stick**
2 teaspoons **chili powder**
1 teaspoon **ground turmeric**
1⅔ cups **reduced-fat**
  coconut milk
salt and **black pepper**

Divide each crab into portions by first removing the main shell. Next, remove the two large claws and use a sharp knife to cut the body into 2 pieces, leaving the legs attached.

Put the onions, garlic, ginger, fenugreek, curry leaves, cinnamon, chile, turmeric, and coconut milk into a large saucepan. Season to taste, then cover and simmer gently for 30 minutes.

Add the crabs to the simmering sauce and cook for 10 minutes to heat through. Serve immediately, with plenty of napkins.

For spicy crab with angel hair pasta, cook 11½ oz angel hair pasta according to package directions. Meanwhile, heat 1 tablespoon peanut oil in a large skillet over a gentle heat and add 3 finely chopped garlic cloves, 1 finely chopped red chile, 6 finely chopped scallions, ⅓ cup reduced-fat coconut milk, and 13 oz white crabmeat. Season and stir-fry for 3–4 minutes. Drain the pasta and add to the crab mixture. Toss to mix well and serve immediately. **Calories per serving 488**

malaysian coconut vegetables

Calories per serving **251**
Serves **4**
Preparation time **15 minutes,
  plus soaking**
Cooking time **20 minutes**

1⅔ cups **broccoli florets**
1¼ cups 1 inch **green bean
  pieces**
1 **red bell pepper**, cored,
  seeded, and sliced
1 small **zucchini**, thinly sliced

Coconut sauce
3 tablespoons **tamarind pulp**
⅔ cup boiling **water**
1⅔ cups **coconut milk**
2 teaspoons **Thai green curry
  paste** (see page 208)
½ inch piece of **fresh ginger
  root**, peeled and finely
  grated
1 **onion**, cut into small cubes
½ teaspoon **ground turmeric**
salt

Make the coconut sauce. Put the tamarind in a bowl. Pour over the measured water and let soak for about 30 minutes. Mash the tamarind in the water, then push through a strainer set over another bowl, squashing the tamarind so that you get as much of the pulp as possible; discard the stringy parts and any seeds.

Take 2 tablespoons of the cream from the top of the coconut milk and pour it into a wok or large skillet. Add the curry paste, ginger, onion, and turmeric, and cook over a gentle heat, stirring, for 2–3 minutes. Stir in the rest of the coconut milk and the tamarind water. Bring to a boil, then reduce the heat to a simmer and add a pinch of salt.

Add the broccoli to the coconut sauce and cook for 5 minutes, then add the green beans and red bell pepper. Cook, stirring, for another 5 minutes. Finally, stir in the zucchini and cook gently for 1–2 minutes, until the zucchini is just tender. Serve immediately with some crispy shrimp crackers, if desired.

For chicken & green beans in coconut sauce,

soak the tamarind and make the coconut sauce as above. Add 1 lb diced boneless, skinless chicken breast to the wok or skillet. Simmer for 5 minutes, then add the sliced green beans, omitting the red bell pepper and zucchini. Simmer gently for another 5 minutes, until the chicken is cooked through. **Calories per serving 365**

recipes
under 400
calories

chicken kofta curry

Calories per serving **343**
Serves **4**
Preparation time **15 minutes**
Cooking time **25 minutes**

1½ lb **ground chicken**
2 teaspoons peeled and finely grated **fresh ginger root**
2 **garlic cloves**, crushed
2 teaspoons **fennel seeds**, crushed
1 teaspoon **ground cinnamon**
1 teaspoon **chili powder**
cooking oil spray
2 cups **tomato puree** or **tomato sauce with onions and garlic**
1 teaspoon **ground turmeric**
2 tablespoons **medium curry powder**
1 teaspoon **agave syrup**
salt and **black pepper**

To serve
½ cup **fat-free plain yogurt**, whisked
pinch of **chili powder**
chopped **mint leaves**

Put the meat into a bowl with the ginger, garlic, fennel seeds, cinnamon, and chili powder. Season to taste and mix thoroughly with your hands until well combined. Form the mixture into walnut-size balls.

Spray a large, nonstick skillet with cooking oil spray and place over medium heat. Add the chicken balls and stir-fry for 4–5 minutes or until lightly browned. Transfer to a plate and keep warm.

Pour the tomato puree or sauce into the skillet and add the turmeric, curry powder, and agave syrup. Bring to a boil, then reduce the heat to a simmer, season to taste, and carefully place the chicken balls in the sauce. Cover and cook gently for 15–20 minutes, turning the balls occasionally, until they are cooked through.

Serve immediately, drizzled with the yogurt and sprinkled with chili powder and mint leaves.

For quick chunky chicken Madras, replace the ground chicken with cubed, boneless, skinless chicken breasts and the medium curry powder with Madras curry powder. Cook as above and add 2 cups peas for the last 5 minutes of cooking. Serve hot. **Calories per serving 387**

spiced squash & spinach soup

Calories per serving **302**
Serves **4**
Preparation time **10 minutes**
Cooking time **30–32 minutes**

2 tablespoons **butter**
2 tablespoons **olive oil**
1 **onion**, coarsely chopped
2 **garlic cloves**, peeled
3 lb **winter squash**, such as
   butternut squash, **acorn
   squash**, or **pumpkin**,
   peeled, seeded, and
   coarsely chopped
1 teaspoon **ground coriander**
½ teaspoon **cayenne pepper**
½ teaspoon **ground
   cinnamon**
¼ teaspoon **ground allspice**
3 cups **hot vegetable stock**
   or **broth**
½ (10 oz) package **frozen
   spinach**
salt and **black pepper**

To serve
2 tablespoons **pumpkin
   seeds**, lightly toasted
4 teaspoons **pumpkin
   seed oil**

Heat the butter and oil in a large, heatproof casserole or Dutch oven and add the onion and garlic. Cook over medium heat for 5–6 minutes, until soft and golden.

Add the squash and continue cooking for another 8 minutes, stirring frequently, until beginning to soften and turn golden. Add the spices and cook for 2–3 minutes, making sure that the squash is well coated.

Pour in the hot stock or broth and bring to a boil, then reduce the heat, cover, and let simmer gently for about 15 minutes, until the squash is soft.

Use a handheld blender to liquidize the squash until smooth, then stir in the spinach. Reheat for about 5 minutes, until the spinach has melted and the soup is hot. Season to taste.

Spoon the soup into bowls, sprinkle with the lightly toasted pumpkin seeds and a drizzle of pumpkin seed oil, and serve immediately.

For squash, spinach & coconut soup, use only 1 lb of winter squash, such as acorn squash, butternut squash, or pumpkin, peeled, seeded, and cubed, and cook as above. Stir in 1 cup reduced-fat coconut milk before serving. **Calories per serving 357**

curried crab & shrimp cakes

Calories per serving **305**
Serves **4**
Preparation time **10 minutes,
  plus chilling**
Cooking time **20–25 minutes**

13 oz **fresh white crabmeat**
13 oz **raw jumbo shrimp**,
  peeled and deveined
1 tablespoon **hot curry
  powder**
2 **garlic cloves**, crushed
1 teaspoon peeled and grated
  fresh ginger root
1 **fresh red chile**, seeded and
  finely chopped
¼ cup finely chopped
  red onion
½ cup chopped **fresh cilantro
  leaves**, plus extra to garnish
1 **medium egg**, beaten
2 cups **fresh whole wheat
  bread crumbs**
cooking oil spray
salt and **black pepper**
lemon wedges, to serve

Put the crabmeat, shrimp, curry powder, garlic, ginger, chile, onion, cilantro, egg, and bread crumbs into a food processor. Season well and pulse for a few seconds until well mixed. Transfer to a bowl, cover, and chill in the refrigerator for 5–6 hours or overnight.

Preheat the oven to 400°F, line a baking sheet with wax paper, and spray with a little cooking oil spray.

Divide the crab mixture into 16 equal portions and shape each into a round cake. Arrange on the prepared baking sheet, spray with a little cooking oil spray, and bake for 20–25 minutes, until lightly browned and cooked through. Garnish with cilantro and serve immediately with lemon wedges.

For piquant crab, shrimp & rice salad, put 13 oz each of fresh white crabmeat and cooked peeled shrimp in a salad bowl with 1¾ cups cold cooked basmati rice or other long-grain rice. Add 6 finely sliced scallions, ½ finely diced cucumber, 10 halved cherry tomatoes, and a small handful of chopped cilantro leaves. In a small bowl, whisk 3 tablespoons light olive oil with ¼ cup lemon juice, 1 teaspoon agave syrup, and 1 finely chopped red chile. Season, pour over the salad, and toss to mix well. **Calories per serving 383**

thai red chicken curry

Calories per serving **307**
Serves **4**
Preparation time **15 minutes**
Cooking time **35 minutes**

1 tablespoon **sunflower oil**
3 **shallots**, finely chopped
3 **garlic cloves**, finely chopped
2 tablespoons **Thai red curry paste**
2 teaspoons **galangal paste**
1⅔ cups **reduced-fat coconut milk**
2 teaspoons **Thai fish sauce**
1 teaspoon **palm sugar** or packed **light brown sugar**
3 **kaffir lime leaves**
6 boneless, skinless **chicken thighs**, diced
handful of **Thai basil leaves** (optional)

Heat the oil in a saucepan over medium heat, add the shallots and garlic, and sauté for 3–4 minutes, until softened. Stir in the curry paste and galangal paste and cook for 1 minute. Mix in the coconut milk, fish sauce, sugar, and lime leaves and bring to a boil.

Stir in the chicken, then reduce the heat, cover, and simmer for 30 minutes, or until the chicken is cooked through, stirring occasionally. Stir in the basil leaves, if using, and serve.

For Thai green chicken curry, make the curry as above, adding 2 peeled and finely chopped lemon grass stalks when frying the shallots and garlic. Replace the red curry paste with 2 tablespoons Thai green curry paste (see page 208 for homemade) and stir in, then continue as above. To finish, stir in the grated zest of 1 lime and lime juice to taste, garnish with chopped cilantro and serve immediately. **Calories per serving 318**

tandoori chicken

Calories per serving **319**
Serves **4**
Preparation time **5 minutes,
 plus marinating**
Cooking time **25–30 minutes**

4 **chicken drumsticks**
4 **chicken thighs**
2 tablespoons **tikka spice mix**
 or **paste**
2 **garlic cloves**, crushed
1 tablespoon **tomato paste**
juice of 1 **lemon**
⅓ cup **plain yogurt**

To garnish
grated **lime** zest
chopped **cilantro**

Make deep slashes all over the chicken pieces. In a large glass or ceramic bowl, mix all the remaining ingredients, then add the chicken and turn to coat thoroughly with the marinade. Cover and let marinate in the refrigerator for at least 30 minutes or overnight.

Transfer the chicken to an ovenproof dish and cook in a preheated oven, at 475°F, for 25–30 minutes, until cooked through, tender, and lightly charred at the edges. Serve garnished with lime zest and chopped cilantro.

For blackened tandoori salmon, use the marinade above to coat 4 thick, skinless salmon fillets (about (6 oz each), then cover and let marinate in the refrigerator for 30 minutes–1 hour. Transfer to a nonstick baking sheet and bake, at 350°F, for 20 minutes or until cooked through. **Calories per serving 377**

cambodian fish curry

Calories per serving **323**
Serves **4**
Preparation time **10 minutes**
Cooking time **15 minutes**

2 tablespoons finely chopped
  lemon grass (tough outer
  leaves removed)
1 tablespoon peeled and finely
  chopped **galangal**
3 **fresh red chiles**, coarsely
  chopped
4 **garlic cloves**, coarsely
  chopped
1 cup **water**
1½ lb thick **halibut fillet**,
  skinned and cubed
1 tablespoon **peanut oil**
1 cup **reduced-fat**
  coconut milk
1 tablespoon **Thai fish sauce**
2 tablespoons chopped
  dry-roasted peanuts
small handful of **Thai basil**
  leaves

Put the lemon grass, galangal, chiles, and garlic into
a mini blender with the measured water and blend
to a smooth paste. Set aside.

Pat the fish dry with paper towels, arrange on a
broiler rack, and cook under a medium-hot broiler for
10–12 minutes or until cooked through.

Meanwhile, heat the oil in a nonstick skillet and stir-fry
the spice paste for 4–5 minutes. Add the coconut milk
and fish sauce and cook, stirring, over a high heat for
5 minutes. Add the fish to the pan with the peanuts and
basil, and toss gently to mix well. Serve immediately.

For spicy fish with lemon grass & coconut, place
4 thick cod fillets in a shallow, lightly greased ovenproof
dish in a single layer. Mix together 2 tablespoons finely
chopped lemon grass, 2 finely chopped fresh red chiles,
2 teaspoons each of grated fresh ginger root and garlic,
and ½ cup reduced-fat coconut milk. Season and spoon
the mixture over the fish. Cook in a preheated oven,
at 350°F, for 15–20 minutes or until cooked through.
Serve garnished with chopped cilantro. **Calories per
serving 182**

spicy marinated lamb chops

Calories per serving **346**
Serves **4**
Preparation time **10 minutes,
   plus marinating**
Cooking time **8–10 minutes**

12 small **lamb chops**, trimmed
½ cup **fat-free plain yogurt**
¼ cup **tomato paste**
¼ cup **medium curry paste**
1 teaspoon grated **garlic**
1 teaspoon peeled and finely
   grated **fresh ginger root**
large pinch of **sea salt**
3 tablespoons **lemon juice**

To serve
1 **red onion**, sliced
4 **tomatoes**, sliced
½ **cucumber**, sliced

Arrange the chops in a single layer in a shallow
nonmetallic dish. Mix the yogurt with the tomato paste,
curry paste, garlic, ginger, sea salt and lemon juice, and
rub into the lamb. Cover and marinate in the refrigerator
for 4–5 hours or overnight.

Preheat the oven to 425°F, and line a large roasting
pan with aluminum foil. Arrange the chops in a single
layer in the pan and cook in the preheated oven for
8–10 minutes, turning halfway through cooking, or
until the lamb is cooked to your preference. Serve
immediately with onion rings along with tomato and
cucumber slices.

For spicy beef skewers, cut 1 ½ lb lean beef
tenderloin into large cubes and put into a nonmetallic
dish. Mix together the marinade as above and pour
it over the beef. Toss to mix well and marinate in the
refrigerator for 6–8 hours or overnight. When ready to
cook, thread the marinated beef onto 8 metal skewers
and broil under a medium-hot broiler for 3–4 minutes
on each side or until cooked to your liking. Serve with
onion rings and tomato and cucumber slices. **Calories
per serving 431**

indonesian yellow drumstick curry

Calories per serving **383**
Serves **4**
Preparation time **15 minutes**
Cooking time **40–45 minutes**

2 **fresh red chiles**, coarsely
chopped, plus extra to garnish
2 **shallots**, coarsely chopped
3 **garlic cloves**, chopped
¼ cup chopped **lemon grass**
(outer leaves removed)
1 tablespoon peeled and finely
chopped **galangal**
2 teaspoons **ground turmeric**
1 teaspoon **cayenne pepper**
1 teaspoon **ground coriander**
1 teaspoon **ground cumin**
¼ teaspoon **ground cinnamon**
3 tablespoons **Thai fish sauce**
1 tablespoon packed **palm
sugar** or **light brown sugar**
4 **kaffir lime leaves**, shredded
1⅔ cups **reduced-fat
coconut milk**
juice of ½ **lime**
8 large **chicken drumsticks**,
skinned
7 oz **baby new potatoes**,
peeled
10–12 **Thai basil leaves**,
to garnish

Put the chiles, shallots, garlic, lemon grass, galangal, turmeric, cayenne, coriander, cumin, cinnamon, fish sauce, sugar, lime leaves, coconut milk, and lime juice into a food processor and blend until fairly smooth.

Arrange the chicken drumsticks in a single layer in an ovenproof casserole or Dutch oven. Spread the potatoes over them. Pour the spice paste over to coat the chicken and potatoes evenly. Cover and cook in a preheated oven, for 40–45 minutes, until the chicken is cooked through and the potatoes are tender. Serve hot, garnished with basil and chopped red chile.

For tandoori drumstick curry, arrange 8 large, skinned chicken drumsticks in a single layer in an ovenproof casserole or Dutch oven. Mix 1¼ cups fat-free plain yogurt with ¼ cup tandoori paste and the juice of 2 lemons. Season and pour the mixture over the chicken to coat evenly. Cover and cook in a preheated oven, at 1350°, for 35–40 minutes, then uncover and continue to cook for 10–15 minutes or until cooked through. Serve warm with a crisp green salad. **Calories per serving 360**

spinach & chicken curry

Calories per serving **351**
Serves **4**
Preparation time **15 minutes,
plus marinating**
Cooking time **1 hour**

⅓ cup **plain yogurt**
2 tablespoons crushed **garlic**
2 tablespoons grated **fresh
ginger root**
1 tablespoon **ground
coriander**
1 tablespoon **mild curry
powder**
1½ lb **boneless, skinless
chicken thighs**, cut into
bite-size pieces
1 (12 oz) package **frozen
whole-leaf spinach**, thawed
2 tablespoons **sunflower oil**
1 **onion**, finely chopped
2 teaspoons **cumin seeds**
½ cup **water**
1 tablespoon **lemon juice**
salt and **black pepper**

Mix together the yogurt, garlic, ginger, ground coriander, and curry powder. Season well. Put the chicken into a large, nonmetallic bowl and pour the yogurt mixture over it Toss to mix well, cover, and marinate in the refrigerator for 8–10 hours.

Put the spinach into a saucepan and cook over medium heat for 6–8 minutes. Season and drain thoroughly. Put the cooked spinach into a food processor and blend until smooth.

Heat the oil in a large nonstick skillet and add the onion. Cook over gentle heat for 10–12 minutes, then add the cumin seeds and stir-fry for 1 minute. Increase the heat to high, add the chicken mixture, and stir-fry for 6–8 minutes. Pour in the measured water and the spinach and bring to a boil.

Reduce the heat to low, cover tightly, and cook for 25–30 minutes or until the chicken is cooked through.

Uncover the pan, check the seasoning, and cook over high heat for 3–4 minutes, stirring constantly. Remove from the heat and stir in the lemon juice. Serve immediately.

For cauliflower & chicken curry, substitute ½ a cauliflower for the spinach. Cut the cauliflower into small florets, halving the larger florets. Proceed as above, adding the cauliflower to the curry when you add the water. **Calories per serving 346**

spiced mussel curry

Calories per serving **353**
Serves **4**
Preparation time **10 minutes**
Cooking time **10–12 minutes**

2 lb **fresh mussels**
1 tablespoon **vegetable oil**
1 **onion**, finely chopped
4 **garlic cloves**, crushed
3 **green chiles**, finely chopped
1 teaspoon **ground turmeric**
½ cup **white wine vinegar**
1⅔ cups **coconut milk**
2 teaspoons **sugar**
¼ cup chopped **fresh cilantro**
salt and **black pepper**
grated fresh coconut or
  unsweetened dried
  coconut, to garnish

Rinse the mussels under cold running water and scrape off any beards. Discard any that are open or that do not close when sharply tapped. Drain and set aside.

Heat the oil in a large saucepan, add the onion, garlic, chiles, and turmeric, and sauté for 2–3 minutes. Add the mussels, vinegar, coconut milk, sugar, and cilantro. Stir well and bring to a boil.

Cover and cook gently for 5–6 minutes or until all the mussels have opened. Discard any that remain shut.

Transfer the mussels to a serving bowl with a slotted spoon, season the cooking juices, and pour the juices over the mussels. Garnish with the coconut and serve.

For sweet & sour mussel curry, add half a pineapple, with woody sections of core removed and the flesh cut into bite-size chunks. Add to the curry at the same time as the mussels and proceed as above. **Calories per serving 369**

balti chicken

Calories per serving **388**
Serves **4**
Preparation time **15 minutes**
Cooking time **20–25 minutes**

1 tablespoon **peanut oil**
2 **onions**, thinly sliced
2 **fresh red chiles**, seeded
  and thinly sliced
6–8 **curry leaves**
1 cup **water**
3 **garlic cloves**, crushed
1 teaspoon peeled and finely
  grated **fresh ginger root**
1 tablespoon **ground
  coriander**
2 tablespoons **Madras curry
  powder**
1 lb **ground chicken**
2⅔ cups **fresh** or **frozen peas**
¼ cup **lemon juice**
small handful of chopped
  mint leaves
small handful of chopped
  fresh cilantro
salt

To serve
chapatis (1 per person)
fat-free plain yogurt
  (2 tablespoons per serving)

Heat the oil in a large wok or skillet over medium heat. Add the onion, chile, and curry leaves, and stir-fry for 4–5 minutes. Add ¼ cup of the measured water and continue to stir-fry for another 2–3 minutes.

Add the garlic, ginger, ground coriander, curry powder, and chicken, and stir-fry over high heat for 10 minutes. Add the remaining measured water and the peas, and continue to cook for 6–8 minutes, until the chicken is cooked through.

Remove from the heat and stir in the lemon juice and herbs. Season to taste, and serve immediately with warmed chapatis and yogurt.

For creamy chicken & vegetable curry, heat 1 tablespoon peanut oil in a large wok or skillet. Add 1 chopped onion, 1 sliced red chile, 6 curry leaves, 2 teaspoons each of crushed fresh ginger root and garlic, and 2 tablespoons mild curry powder. Stir-fry for 1–2 minutes, then add 1¼ lb diced boneless, skinless chicken breasts. Stir-fry for 3–4 minutes, then add 2 cups chicken stock or broth and 1 cup reduced-fat coconut milk. Bring to a boil and cook for 12–15 minutes or until the chicken is cooked through. Stir in 1⅓ cups frozen peas and cook over high heat for 4–5 minutes. Season and serve with rice (about 3 tablespoons per person). **Calories per serving 470**

creamy tandoori chicken kebabs

Calories per serving **356**
Serves **4**
Preparation time **15 minutes,
plus marinating**
Cooking time **6–8 minutes**

1½ lb **boneless, skinless
chicken thighs**, cut into
bite-size pieces
⅔ cup **plain yogurt**, lightly
whisked
½ cup **light cream**
2 teaspoons **crushed garlic**
2 teaspoons grated **fresh
ginger root**
2 tablespoons **medium curry
powder**
¼ cup **garam masala** (see
page 80)
1 teaspoon **ground
cardamom seeds**
2 tablespoons **tomato paste**
¼ cup **lemon juice**
1 tablespoon **tandoori
spice powder**
sunflower oil, for brushing
2 **limes**, halved

Red onion salad
4 **red onions**
salt and **black pepper**
juice of 2 **lemons**

Put the chicken into a large, nonmetallic dish. To make
the marinade, mix together all the remaining ingredients,
season well, and pour over the chicken. Cover and chill
for 24–48 hours.

When ready to cook, let the chicken stand to come to
room temperature.

Meanwhile slice the onions into thin rings and put into
a large mixing bowl. Season with salt and black pepper
and squeeze the juice of the lemons over the top. Cover
and let stand for 30 minutes before tossing and serving
with the kebabs.

Divide the chicken pieces between 8 and 12 metal
skewers, put onto a lightly oiled broiler rack in a single
layer, and lightly brush with sunflower oil.

Put the kebabs under a medium-hot broiler and cook
for 3–4 minutes on each side, or until cooked through.
Alternatively, cook in a preheated oven, at 400°F, for
8–10 minutes. Serve with the red onion salad and lime
halves for squeezing over the kebabs.

For spicy Sunday roast dinner, try marinating a whole
chicken in this creamy marinade. Cover and chill for
24–48 hours, then bring back to room temperature
before roasting it in a preheated oven, at 400°F, for
1¼ hours or until the chicken is cooked through.
Calories per serving 358

stuffed eggplants with lamb

Calories per serving **361**
Serves **4**
Preparation time **20 minutes**
Cooking time **45 minutes**

2 large **eggplants**
1 tablespoon **peanut oil**
1 **onion**, thinly sliced
1 teaspoon peeled and finely
   grated **fresh ginger root**
1 teaspoon **hot chili powder**
1 tablespoon **medium
   curry paste**
2 **garlic cloves**, crushed
¼ teaspoon **ground turmeric**
1 teaspoon **ground coriander**
2 teaspoons **dried mint**
1 **ripe tomato**, finely chopped
1 lb lean **ground lamb**
½ cup finely diced, drained
   roasted red peppers
2 tablespoons chopped **fresh
   cilantro leaves**
2 tablespoons chopped
   mint leaves
salt

Preheat the oven to 350°F. Cut the eggplants in half lengthwise, use a spoon to scoop out most of the flesh, and discard it. Place the eggplants, cut sides up, on a baking sheet and set aside.

Heat the oil in a large skillet over medium heat. Add the onion and stir-fry for 4–5 minutes, until soft. Now add the ginger, chili powder, curry paste, garlic, turmeric, ground coriander, dried mint, and chopped tomato, and stir-fry for 4–5 minutes. Season to taste.

Add the lamb and continue to stir-fry for 5–6 minutes over high heat until well browned. Stir in the roasted red pepper and herbs and mix well. Spoon the lamb mixture into the prepared eggplant shells and cook in the preheated oven for 20–25 minutes. Serve immediately.

For ground lamb & eggplant curry, heat 1 tablespoon peanut oil in a nonstick wok or skillet and add 1 finely chopped onion, 2 crushed garlic cloves, 2 teaspoons grated fresh ginger root, and 2 sliced fresh red chiles, and stir-fry for 3–4 minutes. Cut 1 large eggplant into ¾ inch cubes, add to the pan, and stir-fry for 2–3 minutes. Add 2 tablespoons medium curry powder and 1¼ lb extra-lean ground lamb and stir-fry for 6–8 minutes over high heat until sealed. Stir in 1⅔ cups canned diced tomatoes and 1 teaspoon agave syrup and season to taste. Cook over medium heat for 6–8 minutes or until the lamb is tender and cooked through. Remove from the heat, add a handful each of chopped cilantro and mint leaves, and serve.
Calories per serving 371

pork & lemon grass curry

Calories per serving **362**
Serves **4**
Preparation time **20 minutes**
Cooking time **40 minutes**

¼ cup **sunflower oil**
1½ lb **ground pork**
½ cup finely **chopped lemon grass**
3 **garlic cloves**, crushed
2 teaspoons **grated galangal** or **fresh ginger root**
1 tablespoon **Thai green curry paste** (see page 208)
1 teaspoon **ground turmeric**
2 **fresh green chiles**, chopped
⅔ cup **water**
1⅔ cups **coconut milk**
4 **lime leaves**, finely shredded
3 cups trimmed **sugarsnap peas**
2 tablespoons **lime juice**
salt and **black pepper**

Heat half the oil in a large, nonstick wok and brown the pork over high heat for 3–4 minutes. Remove from the wok and set aside.

Put the lemon grass, garlic, galangal or ginger, curry paste, turmeric, and chiles into a food processor with the measured water and process until smooth.

Add the remaining oil to the wok and place over high heat. Add the lemon grass paste and stir-fry for 2–3 minutes, then add the pork and stir-fry for another 2–3 minutes.

Stir in the coconut milk and lime leaves, season, and bring to a boil. Reduce the heat and simmer, uncovered, for 30 minutes, stirring occasionally.

Add the sugarsnap peas 6 minutes before the end of cooking and stir to mix well.

Remove from the heat and stir in the lime juice before serving.

For pork & vegetable lemon grass curry, use 1½ cups green beans and 5 carrots. Cut the carrots into short thin batons. Cook as above, omitting the sugarsnap peas. **Calories per serving 372**

136

salmon in banana leaves

Calories per serving **366**
Serves **4**
Preparation time **15 minutes**
Cooking time **15 minutes**

large bunch of **fresh cilantro**,
  coarsely chopped
3 tablespoons chopped
mint leaves
2 **garlic cloves**, crushed
1 teaspoon grated **fresh
  ginger root**
4 **fresh red chiles**, seeded
  and chopped
2 teaspoons **ground cumin**
1 teaspoon **ground coriander**
2 teaspoons packed **light
  brown sugar**
2 tablespoons **lime juice**
⅔ cup **coconut milk**
4 **thick salmon fillets**, skinned
4 squares of **banana leaf**
  (about 12 inches square)
salt and **black pepper**

Put the fresh cilantro, mint, garlic, ginger, chiles, cumin, ground coriander, sugar, lime juice, and coconut milk into a food processor or blender and blend until fairly smooth. Season and set aside.

Place each salmon fillet on a square of banana leaf and spoon some of the herb and spice mixture over it. Carefully wrap the fish in the leaf to make a neat package and secure with wooden skewers or toothpicks. If the banana leaves are difficult to handle, dip them in boiling water for 15–20 seconds and they will become more supple.

Place the packages on a large baking sheet and bake in a preheated oven, at 400°F, for 15 minutes.

Remove the packages from the oven, place on a serving plate ,and open the packages at the table.

For swordfish packages, make the packages from parchment paper or aluminum foil instead of banana leaves. Use 4 (6 oz) portions swordfish instead of salmon. Prepare as above and bake in a preheated oven, at 350°F, for 20–25 minutes. **Calories per serving 242**

spicy goan eggplant curry

Calories per serving **367**
Serves **4**
Preparation time **15 minutes**
Cooking time **about**
  25 minutes

1 teaspoon **cumin seeds**
4 teaspoons **coriander seeds**
1 teaspoon **cayenne pepper**
2 **fresh green chiles,** seeded
  and sliced
½ teaspoon **ground turmeric**
4 **garlic cloves,** crushed
1 tablespoon peeled and
  grated **fresh ginger root**
1¼ cups **warm water**
1⅔ cups **reduced-fat**
  coconut milk
1 tablespoon **tamarind paste**
1 large **eggplant,** thinly sliced
  lengthwise
salt and **black pepper**

Dry-roast the cumin and coriander seeds in a nonstick skillet over low heat for 2–3 minutes, until fragrant. Remove from the heat and crush them lightly. Put them into a large saucepan with the cayenne, chiles, turmeric, garlic, ginger, and the measured warm water.

Bring to a boil, reduce the heat, and simmer for 10 minutes, until thickened. Season to taste. Stir in the coconut milk and tamarind paste.

Arrange the eggplant slices in an aluminum foil-lined broiler pan and brush the tops with some of the curry sauce. Cook under a preheated hot broiler, turning once, until golden brown and tender. Serve the eggplant slices in the curry sauce with 1 chapati per person.

For cashew and zucchini curry, add 1⅔ cups roasted cashew nuts to the finished curry sauce. To roast, soak in water for 20 minutes, chop, then heat in a dry skillet, shaking regularly, until lightly browned. Replace the eggplant with 4 sliced zucchini and broil as above. Season to taste. **Calories per serving 438**

bhoona chicken curry

Calories per serving **370**
Serves **4**
Preparation time **10 minutes,
  plus marinating**
Cooking time **8–10 minutes**

½ cup **fat-free plain yogurt**
juice of 2 **limes**
2 **garlic cloves**, finely chopped
1 teaspoon **ground turmeric**
1 tablespoon **mild chili
  powder**
1 teaspoon **cardamom seeds**,
  crushed
large pinch of **sea salt**
1 tablespoon **ground
  coriander**
1 tablespoon **ground cumin**
4 skinless **chicken breasts**,
  cut into strips
1 tablespoon **peanut oil**
1 teaspoon **garam masala**
  (see page 80)
handful of coarsely chopped
  fresh cilantro leaves
¾ cup steamed **rice**
  per person, to serve

Put the yogurt, lime juice, garlic, turmeric, chili powder, cardamom, salt, ground coriander, and cumin into a large nonmetallic bowl. Mix well and add the chicken. Toss to coat evenly, cover, and marinate in the refrigerator for 6–8 hours or overnight.

Heat the oil in a large, nonstick skillet over medium-high heat, and stir-fry the chicken mixture for 8–10 minutes, until tender and cooked through.

Spread over the garam masala and chopped cilantro, stir well, and serve with the steamed rice.

For masala chicken kebabs, prepare the marinade as above and add 4 skinless chicken breasts, cut into cubes. Marinate in the refrigerator for 6–8 hours or overnight if time permits. When ready to cook, thread the chicken pieces onto 8 metal skewers and cook under a medium-hot broiler for 5–6 minutes on each side or until cooked through. Serve with ½ a large, warmed naan per person. **Calories per serving 367**

bangkok sour pork curry

Calories per serving **374**
Serves **4**
Preparation time **20 minutes**
Cooking time **2¼ hours**

1 tablespoon **peanut oil**
1 **onion**, finely chopped
1 teaspoon peeled and finely grated **galangal**
3 tablespoons **Thai red curry paste**
1½ lb thick **pork cutlets**, cubed
3 cups **chicken stock** or **broth**
½ cup finely chopped **fresh cilantro root** and **stem**
2 **lemon grass stalks**, bruised
¼ cup **tamarind paste**
1 tablespoon packed **palm sugar** or **light brown sugar**
6 **kaffir lime leaves**
small handful of **Thai basil leaves**, to garnish

Preheat the oven to 300°F. Heat the oil in a large casserole or Dutch oven and sauté the onion over medium heat for 3–4 minutes. Add the galangal, curry paste, and pork and stir-fry for 4–5 minutes.

Pour in the stock or broth and add the chopped cilantro, lemon grass, tamarind, suga,r and lime leaves. Bring to a boil, cover, and cook in the preheated oven for 2 hours or until the pork is tender.

Garnish with Thai basil and serve.

For Bangkok sour pork curry with noodles, cook 8 oz thick egg noodles according to package directions. Fresh noodles, available in the chilled section of Asian stores and large supermarkets, have the best texture, but dried noodles are a good substitute. Divide the noodles among 4 warmed bowls and ladle the curry, cooked as above, over the top. Sprinkle with chopped cilantro leaves as well as the Thai basil. **Calories per serving 487**

fragrant vietnamese beef curry

Calories per serving **384**
Serves **4**
Preparation time **15 minutes**
Cooking time **20–25 minutes**

2 tablespoons **peanut oil**
1½ lb **thinly sliced beef
tenderloin**, trimmed of fat
and cut into strips
1 **onion**, finely sliced
4 **garlic cloves**, crushed
1 **fresh red chile,** finely sliced
2 **star anise**
1 teaspoon **cardamom seeds**,
crushed
1 **cinnamon stick**
3 cups trimmed **green beans**
1 **carrot**, cut into batons
2 tablespoons **Thai fish sauce**
2 tablespoons **ground bean
sauce**

To garnish
small handful of finely chopped
fresh cilantro leaves
small handful of finely chopped
mint leaves

Heat half the oil in a large, nonstick skillet and stir-fry
the beef in batches for 1–2 minutes. Remove with
a slotted spoon and keep warm.

Heat the remaining oil in the skillet and stir-fry the
onion for 4–5 minutes, until softened, then add the
garlic, chile, star anise, cardamom, cinnamon, beans, and
carrot. Stir-fry for 6–8 minutes.

Return the beef to the pan with the fish sauce and
ground bean sauce. Stir-fry for 3–4 minutes or until
heated through. Remove from the heat and sprinkle
over the chopped herbs just before serving.

For fresh beef spring rolls, soak 8 large rice paper
wrappers in warm water for 3–4 minutes or until soft
and pliable. Pat dry with paper towels and spread
out on a clean work surface. Thinly shred 6 iceberg
lettuce leaves and divide among the wrappers. Top
each with 3 tablespoons of the beef curry, cooked as
above, arranged in a neat pile along the middles of the
wrappers. Turn up the bottom of the wrapper to cover
the filling, then carefully turn the two sides in and gently
roll up. Transfer to a serving plate and cover with a
damp cloth while you make the remaining rolls. Serve
immediately or the wrappers will dry out and become
tough. **Calories per serving 335**

red fish, broccoli, & bean curry

Calories per serving **385**
  (not including rice)
Serves **4**
Preparation time **15 minutes**
Cooking time **10 minutes**

1 tablespoon **peanut oil**
1½–2 tablespoons **Thai red
  curry paste**
1 cup **coconut cream** or
  coconut milk
1 cup **vegetable stock**
  or **broth**
1 tablespoon **tamarind paste**
1 tablespoon **Thai fish sauce**
1 tablespoon packed **palm
  sugar** or light **brown sugar**
3 cups **broccoli florets**
2 cups 1 inch **green bean
  pieces**
14½ oz **thick white fish fillet**,
  skinned and cubed
1 cup drained, canned
  bamboo shoots (optional)
small handful of **Thai basil
  leaves**, to garnish
lime wedges, to serve

Heat the oil in a large wok or skillet over medium heat,
add the curry paste, and stir-fry for 1–2 minutes. Stir
in the coconut cream or milk, stock or broth, tamarind
paste, fish sauce, and sugar and bring to a boil, then
reduce the heat and simmer gently for 2–3 minutes.

Add the broccoli and beans and simmer gently for
2 minutes. Stir in the fish and simmer gently for another
3–4 minutes or until just cooked through. Stir in the
bamboo shoots, if using.

Ladle into warm bowls, sprinkle with Thai basil, and
serve with lime wedges and boiled rice, if desired.

For Thai mixed seafood curry, replace the broccoli
and green beans with 1 large thinly sliced carrot and
1 thinly sliced, seeded red bell pepper. Follow the recipe
above, omitting the fish, but adding 12 raw jumbo
shrimp, peeled and deveined, 4 oz prepared squid rings,
and 1 lb scrubbed and debearded mussels. Simmer
gently until the mussels open, discarding any that do
not. Add 1¼ cups fresh or canned pineapple chunks
instead of the bamboo shoots and serve as above.
Calories per serving 368 (not including rice)

thai jungle curry with duck

Calories per serving **389**
Serves **4**
Preparation time **20 minutes**
Cooking time **30 minutes**

2 tablespoons **Thai green curry paste** (see page 208)
2 tablespoons finely chopped **lemon grass** (tough outer leaves removed)
3 **kaffir lime leaves**, finely shredded
1 teaspoon **shrimp paste**
6 **garlic cloves**, crushed
5 **shallots**, finely chopped
3 tablespoons finely chopped **cilantro root**
2 tablespoons **peanut oil**
cooking oil spray
1¼ lb **skinless duck breast**, thinly sliced
1⅔ cups **chicken stock** or **broth**
1 tablespoon **Thai fish sauce**
½ cup rinsed and drained, canned **bamboo shoots**
4 **baby eggplants**, quartered
small handful of **Thai basil leaves**

Put the green curry paste, lemon grass, lime leaves, shrimp paste, garlic, shallots, cilantro root, and peanut oil into a mini blender and blend to a smooth paste, adding a little water, if necessary.

Spray a large, nonstick wok with cooking oil spray, place over high heat, and add the curry paste. Stir-fry for 1–2 minutes, then add the duck. Stir-fry for 4–5 minutes, until sealed, then pour in the stock or broth and fish sauce and bring to a boil. Remove the duck from the pan with a slotted spoon, set aside, and keep warm.

Add the bamboo shoots and eggplants to the pan and cook for 12–15 minutes or until tender.

Return the meat to the pan and cook gently for 3–4 minutes. Stir in half the basil leaves and remove from the heat. Ladle into bowls, and garnish with the remaining basil.

For jungle curry with pigeon, replace the duck with 8 pigeon breasts, thinly sliced. Follow the recipe above, using light soy sauce instead of Thai fish sauce, and replacing the bamboo shoots with canned water chestnuts for a crunchy texture. Cook as above until the pigeon is tender. **Calories per serving 409**

curried tofu with vegetables

Calories per serving **393**
Serves **4**
Preparation time **20 minutes**
Cooking time **25 minutes**

2 tablespoons **sunflower oil**
2 teaspoons finely **grated fresh ginger root**
8 **garlic cloves**, chopped
8 **small shallots**, chopped
1 teaspoon **ground turmeric**
2 **fresh red chiles**, chopped
¼ cup finely chopped **lemon grass**
1⅔ cups **coconut milk**
1 cup **vegetable stock** or **broth**
4 **lime leaves**, finely shredded
12 **baby zucchini**, cut in half lengthwise
12 **baby corn**, trimmed and cut in half lengthwise
13 oz **firm tofu**, cut into bite-size cubes
1 tablespoon **dark soy sauce**
1 tablespoon **lime juice**
salt and **black pepper**
small handful of coarsely chopped **fresh cilantro**

Put the oil, ginger, garlic, shallots, turmeric, chiles, lemon grass, and half the coconut milk into a food processor and process until fairly smooth.

Heat a large, nonstick wok or skillet and pour the coconut mixture into it. Stir-fry over high heat for 3–4 minutes, then add the remaining coconut milk, the stock or broth, and lime leaves. Bring to a boil, reduce the heat, and simmer gently, uncovered, for 10 minutes.

Add the zucchini and baby corn to the mixture and simmer for 6–7 minutes. Stir in the tofu, soy sauce, and lime juice, season to taste, and cook gently for 1–2 minutes.

Remove from the heat and stir in the fresh cilantro. Serve in bowls garnished with basil leaves.

For pattypan curry with seafood, replace the baby zucchini and corn with pattypan squash, and use reduced-fat coconut milk. Cook as above. Replace the tofu with 16–20 raw jumbo shrimp and 1 lb squid rings. Add the shrimp and squid to the curry with the vegetables and finish as above. **Calories per serving 343**

cumin lentils with yogurt dressing

Calories per serving **398**
Serves **4**
Preparation time **10 minutes**
Cooking time **13 minutes**

¼ cup **olive oil**
2 **red onions**, thinly sliced
2 **garlic cloves**, chopped
2 teaspoons **cumin seeds**
2½ cups cooked **Puy lentils**
  or **other green lentils**
4 cups **peppery salad leaves**,
  such as beet or arugula
1 large **raw beet**, peeled and
  coarsely grated
1 **Granny Smith apple** or
  other **cooking apple**,
  peeled and coarsely grated
  (optional)
lemon juice, to serve
salt and **black pepper**

Yogurt dressing
1¼ cups **Greek yogurt**
2 tablespoons **lemon juice**
½ teaspoon **ground cumin**
¼ cup chopped **mint leaves**

Heat the oil in a skillet and sauté the red onions over medium heat for about 8 minutes, until soft and golden brown. Add the garlic and cumin seeds and cook for another 5 minutes.

Mix the onion mixture into the lentils, season well, and let cool.

Make the yogurt dressing by mixing together the ingredients in a small bowl.

Serve the cooled lentils on a bed of greens, with the grated beet and apple (if used), a couple of spoonfuls of minty yogurt, and a generous squeeze of lemon juice.

For cumin chickpeas with apricots, use 5½ cups rinsed and drained, canned chickpeas instead of the lentils. Chop and add ¾ cup dried apricots to replace the beet and apple. **Calories per serving 414**

monkfish & sweet potato curry

Calories per serving **399**
  (not including rice)
Serves **4**
Preparation time **15 minutes**
Cooking time **about
  20 minutes**

2 **lemon grass stalks**,
  coarsely chopped
2 **shallots**, coarsely chopped
1 **large red chile**, seeded
1 **garlic clove**
(¾ inch piece of **fresh ginger
  root**, peeled and chopped
3 tablespoons **peanut oil**
3⅓ cups **reduced-fat
  coconut milk**
2 **sweet potatoes**, peeled and
  cut into ¾ inch cubes
2 **large monkfish tails**
  (about 8 oz each), cut into
  large chunks
2 tablespoons **Thai fish sauce**
1 teaspoon packed **dark
  brown sugar**
1½ tablespoons **lime juice**
2 tablespoons coarsely
  chopped **fresh cilantro**,
  to garnish

Put the lemon grass, shallots, chile, garlic, ginger, and oil in a food processor or blender and blend to a smooth paste.

Heat a saucepan over medium heat, add the paste, and cook for 2 minutes, until fragrant, then add the coconut milk. Bring to a boil and cook for 5 minutes, until it reaches the consistency of cream. Add the sweet potatoes and cook until almost tender.

Add the monkfish and simmer for another 5 minutes or until the fish is firm and cooked through. Add the fish sauce, sugar, and lime juice, to taste. Sprinkle with the cilantro. Serve with some Thai sticky rice, if desired.

For Thai-roasted monkfish with roasted chile
squash, mix 2 tablespoons Thai red curry paste with ¼ cup fat-free plain yogurt in a nonmetallic bowl. Add 2 monkfish tails, cut into large pieces, cover, and let marinate in the refrigerator for at least 20 minutes or overnight, if possible. Pan-fry the pieces of fish in a little vegetable oil until cooked through. Scoop out the seeds from ½ butternut squash or 1 lb of other pumpkin or winter squash, peel, and cut into 1 inch cubes. Sprinkle with dried red pepper flakes and roast in a preheated oven, at 400°F, for 15–20 minutes, or until tender, turning occasionally. Serve with extra plain yogurt mixed with chopped cilantro. **Calories per serving 177**

thai red tofu & vegetable curry

Calories per serving **364**
  (not including rice)
Serves **4**
Preparation time **15 minutes**
Cooking time **25–30 minutes**

14½ oz **firm tofu**
1 tablespoon **canola oil**
2 tablespoons **Thai red
  curry paste**
1–2 **fresh green chiles**, sliced
1 cup **reduced-fat coconut
  milk**
1 cup **vegetable stock**
  or **broth**
1 large **eggplant**, diced
12 **baby corn**
1½ cups **snow peas**
2 **carrots**, sliced
4 oz **shiitake mushrooms**,
  halved
1 large **green bell pepper**,
  sliced
1 cup drained, canned **sliced
  bamboo shoots**
1 tablespoon **Thai fish sauce**
1 tablespoon **honey**
2 **kaffir lime leaves**

To garnish
handful of **Thai basil leaves**
handful of **cashew nuts**,
  toasted

Drain the tofu and pat it dry with paper towels before cutting it into 2 inch cubes.

Heat the oil in a wok over high heat until the oil starts to shimmer. Stir-fry the red curry paste and chiles for 1 minute, then stir in 2 tablespoons of the coconut milk (from the thicker part at the top of the can) and cook, stirring constantly, for 2 minutes.

Add the stock and bring to a boil. Add the eggplant, then bring the mixture back to a boil and simmer for about 5 minutes. Add the remaining vegetables and cook for another 5–10 minutes. Stir in the fish sauce, honey, lime leaves, and the remaining coconut milk and simmer for another 5 minutes, stirring occasionally. Add the tofu cubes and mix well.

Garnish with torn Thai basil leaves and toasted cashew nuts. Serve with jasmine or glutinous rice, if desired, which will absorb the wonderful aromatic sauce.

For one-dish tofu & vegetable noodles, use 1⅔ cups reduced-fat coconut milk and increase the quantity of stock or broth to 1½ cups. Add 2 oz thick rice noodles, cooked, along with the tofu and simmer for 1 minute before serving with the garnish above. **Calories per serving 499**

curried cauliflower with chickpeas

Calories per serving **310**
  (not including chapatis)
Serves **4**
Preparation time **10 minutes**
Cooking time **20 minutes**

2 tablespoons **olive oil**
1 **onion**, chopped
2 **garlic cloves**, crushed
¼ cup **medium curry paste**
1 small **cauliflower,** divided
  into florets
1½ cups **vegetable stock**
  or **broth**
4 **tomatoes**, coarsely chopped
1⅔ cups rinsed and drained,
  canned **chickpeas**
2 tablespoons **mango
  chutney** (see right)
salt and **black pepper**
¼ cup chopped **fresh cilantro**,
  to garnish

Heat the oil in a saucepan, add the onion and garlic, and cook until the onion is soft and starting to brown. Stir in the curry paste, add the cauliflower and stock or broth, and bring to a boil. Reduce the heat, cover tightly, and simmer for 10 minutes.

Add the tomatoes, chickpeas, and chutney and continue to cook, uncovered, for 10 minutes. Season to taste with salt and black pepper. Garnish with cilantro and serve with rolled chapatis, if desired.

For homemade mango chutney, put the peeled, pitted, and sliced flesh of 6 ripe mangoes in a large saucepan with 1¼ cups white wine vinegar and cook over low heat for 10 minutes. Add 1¼ cups packed dark brown sugar, ½ cup peeled and finely chopped, fresh ginger root, 2 crushed garlic cloves, 2 teaspoons chili powde,r and 1 teaspoon salt and bring to a boil, stirring constantly. Reduce the heat and simmer for 30 minutes, stirring occasionally. Ladle into a sterilized screw-top jar and replace the lid. Store in the refrigerator and use within 1 month. **Calories per jar 449**

spiced beef & vegetable stew

Calories per serving **325**
Serves **4**
Preparation time **15 minutes**
Cooking time **2½ hours**

1 lb **boneless beef chuck** or **beef round**

2 tablespoons **canola** or **olive oil**

1 large **onion**, chopped

1 inch piece of **fresh ginger root**, peeled and finely grated

2 **chiles**, sliced

2 **garlic cloves**, crushed

2½ cups **beef stock** or **broth**

5 **star anise**

1 teaspoon **Chinese five-spice powder**

1 **cinnamon stick**

1 teaspoon **fennel seeds**

2 **dried kaffir lime leaves**

1 **lemon grass stalk**, chopped

1 teaspoon **black peppercorns**

2 tablespoons **shoyu** or **tamari sauce**

7 **carrots**, cut into ½ inch slices

1 lb **daikon radish** or **turnips**, cut into ½ inch slices

Chinese chives or **regular chives**, to garnish

Cut the beef into 1 inch cubes.

Heat the oil in a wok over medium heat. Add the onion, ginger, and chiles and stir-fry for 5–7 minutes.

Turn the heat up to high, add the beef, and stir-fry for 5–10 minutes, until lightly browned, stirring occasionally.

Add the garlic, stock, star anise, Chinese five-spice powder, cinnamon, fennel seeds, lime leaves, lemon grass, peppercorns, and shoyu sauce and stir well. Bring the mixture back to a boil, then turn the heat down, cover the pan, and simmer gently for 1½ hours, stirring occasionally. Add the carrots and daikon and continue cooking, covered, for another 45 minutes or until the vegetables have softened.

Skim any fat off the surface and garnish with the chives before serving.

For sesame broccoli, to accompany the stew, blanch 7 cups broccoli florets in a saucepan of boiling water for 2 minutes, then drain and place on a serving dish. Make a dressing by combining 1 teaspoon sesame oil, 1 tablespoon shoyu sauce, and 1 crushed garlic clove, and pour it over the broccoli. Just before serving, sprinkle the dish with 1 tablespoon toasted sesame seeds. **Calories per serving 69**

strawberry lassi

Approximate calories per
serving **375**
Makes **6⅓ cups**

13 oz **strawberries**
3 cups **ice-cold water**
1¼ cups **low-fat plain yogurt**
2 tablespoons **sugar**
few drops of **rose water**
coarsely ground **black pepper**,
to serve

Hull and coarsely chop the strawberries. Put the strawberries into a food processor or blender with half the water and process until smooth.

Add the yogurt, sugar, rose water, and the remaining water and process again until smooth and frothy.

Pour the smoothie into chilled glasses, sprinkle with black pepper, and serve immediately.

For banana lassi, process 2 small ripe bananas with 1¼ cups plain yogurt, ½ cup ice-cold water and a pinch of ground cardamom in a food processor or blender. **Calories per 6 servings 382**

recipes
under 500
calories

spiced halibut curry

Calories per serving **404**
(**not including yogurt**)
Serves **4**
Preparation time **15 minutes,
plus chilling**
Cooking time **40–50 minutes**

¼ cup **lemon juice**
¼ cup **rice wine vinegar**
2 tablespoons **cumin seeds**
1 teaspoon **chili powder**
1 teaspoon **ground turmeric**
1 teaspoon **salt**
1½ lb thick **halibut fillets,**
skinned and cut into cubes
¼ cup **sunflower oil**
1 **onion**, finely chopped
3 **garlic cloves**, crushed
2 tablespoons finely grated
fresh ginger root
2 teaspoons **black mustard
seeds**
3⅓ cups canned **diced
tomatoes**
1 teaspoon **sugar**

To garnish
chopped **fresh cilantro**
sliced **fresh green chiles**
plain yogurt (optional)

Mix together the lemon juice, rice wine vinegar, cumin, chili powder, turmeric, and salt in a nonmetallic bowl. Add the fish and turn to coat evenly. Cover and chill for 25–30 minutes.

Meanwhile, heat a wok over high heat and add the oil. When hot, add the onion, garlic, ginger, and mustard seeds. Reduce the heat and cook gently for 10 minutes, stirring occasionally.

Add the tomatoes and sugar, bring to a boil, reduce the heat, cover, and cook gently for 15–20 minutes, stirring occasionally.

Add the fish and its marinade, stir gently to mix, then cover and simmer gently for 15–20 minutes or until the fish is cooked through and flakes easily.

Garnish with chopped fresh cilantro and green chiles and drizzle with some plain yogurt, if desired.

For dry-spiced cod, use 1½ lb cod fillets instead of halibut, cutting the fillets into large chunks. Heat a wok over high heat and pour in the sunflower oil. When hot, add the onion, garlic, fresh ginger root, and black mustard seeds. Add the fish and cook for 5 minutes, until just firm, turning occasionally. Add 2–3 tablespoons water and cook for 3–5 minutes. Serve drizzled with yogurt, if desired, and sprinkled with cilantro. **Calories per serving 307 (not including yogurt)**

monkfish korma

Calories per serving **405**
Serves **4**
Preparation time **10 minutes**
Cooking time **20 minutes**

1 tablespoon **peanut oil**
2 tablespoons **korma curry powder**
1½ lb **monkfish fillet**, cubed
large bunch of **fresh cilantro leaves**, finely chopped
1 **red onion**, finely chopped
finely grated zest and juice of 2 **limes**
1⅔ cups canned **reduced-fat coconut milk**
salt and **black pepper**
¾ cup steamed **rice** per person, to serve

Heat the oil in a wide saucepan over medium heat. Add the curry powder and stir-fry for 20–30 seconds or until fragrant. Add the monkfish, cilantro, and red onion and cook, stirring, for another 20–30 seconds.

Add the lime zest and juice and the coconut milk. Bring to a boil, reduce the heat, and simmer for 15 minutes or until the fish is cooked through. Season to taste and serve immediately with the steamed rice.

For monkfish Madras, replace the korma curry powder with Madras curry powder, and the coconut milk with 1 cup tomato puree or tomato sauce and 1 cup fish stock or broth. Cook as above until the fish is cooked through. Serve with 1 chapati per person. **Calories per serving 451**

sri lankan-style lamb curry

Calories per serving **409**
Serves **4**
Preparation time **10 minutes**
Cooking time **35 minutes**

1 lb **boneless shoulder** or **leg of lamb**, diced
2 **potatoes**, peeled and cut into large chunks
¼ cup **olive oil**
1⅔ cups canned **diced tomatoes**
⅔ cup **water**
salt and **black pepper**

Curry paste
1 **onion**, grated
1 tablespoon peeled and finely chopped **fresh ginger root**
1 teaspoon minced **garlic**
½ teaspoon **ground turmeric**
1 teaspoon **ground coriander**
½ teaspoon **ground cumin**
½ teaspoon **fennel seeds**
½ teaspoon **cumin seeds**
3 **cardamom pods**, crushed
2 **fresh green chiles**, finely diced
2 inch **cinnamon stick**
2 **lemon grass stalks**, thinly sliced

Make the curry paste. Mix together all the ingredients in a large bowl. (For a milder curry, remove the seeds from the chiles before dicing.) Add the lamb and potatoes and mix well.

Heat the oil in a heavy saucepan, Dutch oven, or flameproof casserole, add the lamb and potato mixture, and cook, stirring, for 6–8 minutes.

Stir in the tomatoes and measured water and bring to a boil. Season well with salt and black pepper, then reduce the heat and simmer for 20–25 minutes, until the potatoes are cooked and the lamb is tender.

For beef & potato curry, use 1 lb top sirloin steak, cut into chunks, instead of the lamb. Cook the recipe as above and then serve with a generous sprinkling of chopped fresh cilantro. **Calories per serving 435**

swahili chicken

Calories per serving **412 (not including rice or flatbread)**
Serves **4**
Preparation time **20 minutes, plus marinating**
Cooking time **1½ hours**

1 **chicken**, cut into 8 pieces
4 teaspoons finely **grated fresh ginger root**
6 **garlic cloves**, crushed
2 teaspoons **ground turmeric**
1 tablespoon **paprika**
1 teaspoon **ground cinnamon**
½ cup **lemon juice**
¼ cup **sunflower oil**
2 teaspoons **ground cumin**
1 tablespoon **ground coriander**
2 teaspoons **dried red pepper flakes**
½ cup **plain yogurt**, whisked
1 tablespoon **honey**
salt and **black pepper**

Put the chicken pieces into a large mixing bowl. Mix together the remaining ingredients, season well, and pour the marinade over the chicken. Mix well to combine, cover, and marinate in the refrigerator for 6–8 hours or overnight if time permits.

Put the chicken mixture into a shallow, lightly oiled, ovenproof baking dish and cook in a preheated oven, at 300°F, for 1½ hours, covering the dish with aluminum foil for the last 30–40 minutes of cooking. Serve accompanied by plain boiled rice or flatbread, if desired.

For Swahili chicken drumsticks with cumin dip,

use 12 small chicken drumsticks instead of the whole chicken and proceed as above. To make it easier to eat the drumsticks with your fingers, only cover the chicken with aluminum foil when the dish is dry. Serve at room temperature with minted yogurt for dipping. To make it, whisk 1 cup plain yogurt with ¼ teaspoon ground cumin and ¼ cup finely chopped fresh mint. Season well, then chill until ready to serve. **Calories per serving 405**

fast chicken curry

Calories per serving **413**
Serves **4**
Preparation time **5 minutes**
Cooking time **20–25 minutes**

3 tablespoons **olive oil**
1 **onion**, finely chopped
¼ cup **medium curry paste**
8 boneless, skinless **chicken thighs**, cut into thin strips
1⅔ cups canned **diced tomatoes**
½ **head of broccoli**, broken into small florets, stems peeled and sliced
½ cup **reduced-fat coconut milk**
salt and **black pepper**

Heat the oil in a deep, nonstick saucepan over medium heat. Add the onion and cook for 3 minutes, until soft and translucent. Add the curry paste and cook, stirring, for 1 minute until fragrant.

Add the chicken, tomatoes, broccoli, and coconut milk to the pan. Bring to a boil, then reduce the heat, cover, and simmer gently over low heat for 15–20 minutes, until the chicken is cooked through.

Remove from the heat, season well with salt and black pepper, and serve immediately.

For chicken patties with curry sauce, follow the first stage of the recipe above, then add the tomatoes, 7 cups young spinach leaves, and the reduced-fat coconut milk (omitting the chicken and broccoli), and cook as directed. Meanwhile, finely chop 3 cups cooked chicken breast pieces. Transfer to a bowl and add 4 finely chopped scallions, 2 tablespoons chopped fresh cilantro, 1 cup fresh white bread crumbs, a squeeze of lemon juice, and 1 beaten egg. Season with salt and black pepper. Mix well, then form into 16 patties. Roll in ½ cup fresh white bread crumbs to coat. Brush vegetable oil around a large skillet over medium heat. Add the patties, cooking in batches, and pan-fry on each side until golden brown and cooked through. Serve hot with the curry sauce. **Calories per serving 490**

chicken & baby spinach curry

Calories per serving **420**
Serves **4**
Preparation time **10 minutes**
Cooking time **25 minutes**

1 tablespoon **sunflower oil**
4 **boneless, skinless chicken
   breasts**, halved lengthwise
1 **onion**, sliced
2 **garlic cloves**, chopped
1 **green chile,** chopped
4 **cardamom pods,**
   lightly crushed
1 teaspoon **cumin seeds**
1 teaspoon **dried red
   pepper flakes**
1 teaspoon **ground ginger**
1 teaspoon **ground turmeric**
8 cups **baby leaf spinach**
3 **tomatoes**, chopped
⅔ cup **plain yogurt**
2 tablespoons chopped
   fresh cilantro
¾ cup steamed **rice** per
   person, to serve

Heat the oil in a large, nonstick saucepan or skillet. Add the chicken, onion, garlic, and chile and sauté for 4–5 minutes, until the chicken begins to brown and the onion to soften.

Add the cardamom pods, cumin seeds, red pepper flakes, ginger, and turmeric and continue to cook for 1 minute.

Add the spinach to the pan, cover, and cook gently until the spinach wilts, then stir in the tomatoes and simmer for 15 minutes, removing the lid for the last 5 minutes.

Stir in the yogurt and chopped cilantro and serve with the steamed rice.

For chicken & pea curry, use 1⅓ cups fresh or frozen peas, adding them to the curry with the tomatoes. Sprinkle with 1 tablespoon chopped fresh mint as well as the cilantro before serving. **Calories per serving 458**

curry leaf & tomato shrimp

Calories per serving **427**
Serves **4**
Preparation time **15 minutes**
Cooking time **15–20 minutes**

1 tablespoon **peanut oil**
10–12 **curry leaves**
2 large shallots, halved and
   finely sliced
2 teaspoons finely grated
   garlic
1 teaspoon peeled and finely
   grated **fresh ginger root**
1 tablespoon **fennel seeds**
1 tablespoon **medium curry
   powder**
6 **large ripe tomatoes**,
   peeled, seeded, and
   chopped
1½ lb **raw jumbo shrimp**,
   peeled and deveined
salt
¾ cup steamed **rice** per
   person, to serve

Heat the oil in a large wok or skillet over medium heat. Add the curry leaves and stir-fry for 30 seconds. Add the shallots and stir-fry for another 4–5 minutes.

Add the garlic, ginger, and fennel seeds, reduce the heat, and cook gently for 2–3 minutes. Sprinkle with the curry powder and add the tomatoes, including any juices. Increase the heat and stir-fry for 3–4 minutes.

Add the shrimp and continue cooking over high heat for 6–7 minutes, until the shrimp turn pink and are just cooked through. Remove from the heat, season to taste, and serve immediately with the rice or crushed sesame spiced potatoes.

For crushed sesame spiced potatoes, to serve as an accompaniment, peel 4 medium potatoes and cut into ½ inch dice. Boil for 12 minutes or until just tender, then drain thoroughly. Heat 1 tablespoon peanut oil in a large skillet over high heat. Add 1 tablespoon sesame seeds, 2 teaspoons cumin seeds, 2 teaspoons red chili powder, ¼ teaspoon ground turmeric, and the potatoes and stir-fry for 6–8 minutes, crushing them lightly with the back of a spoon. Season and serve. **Calories per serving 366**

burmese chicken noodle curry

Calories per serving **403**
Serves **6**
Preparation time **20 minutes**
Cooking time **about 1 hour**

2 lb boneless, skinless
   chicken thighs, cut into
   bite-size pieces
2 **onions**, chopped
5 **garlic cloves**, chopped
1 teaspoon finely grated **fresh
   ginger root**
2 tablespoons **sunflower oil**
½ teaspoon **Burmese shrimp
   paste** (belacan)
1⅔ cups **coconut milk**
1 tablespoon **medium curry
   powder**
10½ oz **dried rice vermicelli**
salt and **black pepper**

To garnish
chopped **fresh cilantro**
finely chopped **red onion**
fried **garlic slivers**
sliced **fresh red chiles**
lime wedges

Season the chicken pieces and set aside. Process the onion, garlic, and ginger in a food processor until smooth. If necessary, add a little water to assist in blending the mixture. Heat the oil in a large saucepan. Add the onion mixture and shrimp paste and cook, stirring, over high heat for about 5 minutes.

Add the chicken and cook over medium heat, turning it until it browns.

Pour in the coconut milk and add the curry powder. Bring to a boil, reduce the heat, and simmer, covered, for about 30 minutes, stirring from time to time. Uncover the pan and cook for another 15 minutes or until the chicken is tender and cooked through.

Put the noodles into a bowl, cover with boiling water, and set aside for 10 minutes. Drain the noodles and divide them among 4 large, warm serving bowls. Ladle the curry over the noodles, and garnish with chopped cilantro, chopped red onion, fried garlic slivers, sliced red chiles, and lime wedges.

For tofu noodle curry, replace the chicken with 14½ oz cubed tofu, then add 4 baby corn and 1 cup snow peas to the curry 5 minutes before the end of cooking. Finish as above. **Calories per serving 313**

malay beef with peanut sauce

Calories per serving **435**
Serves **6**
Preparation time **10 minutes**
Cooking time **15 minutes**

1 lb **tenderloin** or **top sirloin steak**, thinly sliced
1 tablespoon **vegetable oil**

Marinade
½ teaspoon **turmeric**
1 teaspoon **ground cumin**
½ teaspoon **fennel seeds**
1 **bay leaf**, finely shredded
½ teaspoon **ground cinnamon**
⅓ cup **coconut cream** or **coconut milk**

Rice
1½ cups **jasmine rice**
1 cup **reduced-fat coconut milk**
½ teaspoon **salt**

Peanut sauce
2 tablespoons **chunky peanut butter**
¼ teaspoon **cayenne pepper**
1 tablespoon **light soy sauce**
½ cup **coconut cream** or **coconut milk**
½ teaspoon **sugar**

Make the marinade by mixing together all the ingredients in a nonmetallic bowl. Add the beef, mix thoroughly, then thread the beef onto skewers and set aside to marinate.

Put the rice, coconut milk, salt, and 1 cup water in a rice cooker or a covered saucepan over low heat. Cook for about 15 minutes, until the rice is cooked and the liquid has been absorbed.

Meanwhile, add the ingredients for the peanut sauce to a small saucepan with 3 tablespoons water and heat gently, stirring.

Heat the oil in a large skillet and cook the beef skewers for about 5 minutes, turning so that each side is browned evenly. Serve immediately with the rice and peanut sauce.

For bean sprout & carrot salad to serve as an accompaniment, coarsely grate 4 carrots, coarsely chop 4 scallions, and combine with 2 cups bean sprouts. **Calories per serving 58**

spicy cod & tomato curry

Calories per serving **435**
Serves **4**
Preparation time **15 minutes**
Cooking time **40–50 minutes**

¼ cup **lemon juice**
¼ cup **rice wine vinegar**
2 tablespoons **cumin seeds**
2 tablespoons **hot curry powder**
large pinch of **salt**
1½ lb thick **cod fillet**, skinned and cubed
1 tablespoon **peanut oil**
1 **onion**, finely chopped
3 **garlic cloves**, finely chopped
2 teaspoons peeled and finely grated **fresh ginger root**
3⅓ cups canned **diced tomatoes**
1 teaspoon **agave syrup**
¾ cup boiled **rice** per person, to serve

Mix the lemon juice with the rice wine vinegar, cumin seeds, curry powder, and salt in a shallow, nonmetallic bowl. Add the fish and turn to coat evenly. Cover and marinate in the refrigerator for 25–30 minutes.

Meanwhile, heat a wok or large skillet with a lid over high heat and add the oil. When the oil is hot, add the onion, garlic, and ginger. Reduce the heat and cook gently for 10 minutes, stirring occasionally.

Add the tomatoes and agave syrup, stir well, and bring to a boil. Reduce the heat, cover, and cook gently for 15–20 minutes, stirring occasionally.

Add the fish and its marinade, and stir gently to mix. Cover and simmer gently for 15–20 minutes, until the fish is cooked through. Ladle into shallow bowls and serve with a boiled rice.

For cod & tomato biryani, put 1 tablespoon medium curry powder into a medium saucepan with 1 bay leaf, 1 cinnamon stick, a large pinch of saffron, 4 crushed cardamom pods, 3 cloves, ⅓ cup tomato paste, and 1½ cups basmati rice or other long grain rice. Pour in 2¾ cups hot fish stock or broth, season, and stir to mix well. Bring back to a boil and gently stir in 13 oz skinless cod fillet chunks. Reduce the heat to low, cover the pan, and cook gently for 10–12 minutes or until all the liquid has been absorbed. Remove from the heat and let stand, covered and undisturbed, for 10–15 minutes. Fluff up the grains with a fork and serve. **Calories per serving 413**

thai monkfish & shrimp curry

Calories per serving **446**
Serves **4**
Preparation time **10 minutes**
Cooking time **8 minutes**

3 tablespoons **Thai green
curry paste** (see page 208)
1⅔ cups **reduced-fat
coconut milk**
1 **lemon grass stalk**
(optional), halved lengthwise
2 **kaffir lime leaves** (fresh or
dried, optional)
1 tablespoon packed **light
brown sugar**
10 oz **monkfish or cod loins,**
cubed
½ cup trimmed **green beans**
12 raw peeled **jumbo shrimp**
2–3 tablespoons **Thai fish
sauce**
2 tablespoons fresh **lime juice**
¾ cup boiled **rice** per person,
to serve

To garnish
fresh cilantro sprigs
sliced **fresh green chiles**

Put the curry paste and coconut milk into a saucepan.
Bruise the lemon grass stalk by banging it with a rolling
pin, and add it to the pan with lime leaves, if using, and
sugar. Bring to a boil, then add the monkfish. Simmer
gently for 2 minutes, then add the beans and cook for
another 2 minutes or until the fish is cooked through.

Stir in the shrimp, fish sauce, and lime juice and cook
for 2–5 minutes, until the shrimp turn pink and are
cooked through.

Transfer the curry to a warm serving dish and top
with cilantro sprigs and chili slices. Serve with plain
boiled rice.

For Malaysian monkfish & shrimp curry, heat
2 tablespoons sunflower oil in a saucepan, add 2 thinly
sliced onions, and sauté gently until softened. Replace
the curry paste with 2 tablespoons lemon grass paste,
1 tablespoon garlic paste, 1 seeded and diced red chile,
1¾ inch piece of fresh ginger root, peeled and grated,
1 teaspoon turmeric, 1 cinnamon stick, and 2 star anise
and add to the onions with the reduced-fat coconut
milk, lemon grass, and lime leaves, if using, sugar, and
salt. Continue as above. **Calories per serving 461**

mango & shrimp curry

Calories per serving **447**
Serves **4**
Preparation time **10 minutes**
Cooking time **20–25 minutes**

3 **garlic cloves**, crushed
2 teaspoons peeled and finely grated **fresh ginger root**
2 tablespoons **ground coriander**
2 teaspoons **ground cumin**
1 teaspoon **chili powder**
1 teaspoon **paprika**
½ teaspoon **ground turmeric**
1 tablespoon packed **palm sugar** or **light brown sugar**
1⅔ cups **water**
1 **green mango**, peeled, pitted, and thinly sliced
1⅔ cups **reduced-fat coconut milk**
1 tablespoon **tamarind paste**
1¼ lb raw **jumbo shrimp**, peeled and deveined
small bunch of **fresh cilantro**
salt
¾ cup boiled **rice** per person, to serve

Put the garlic, ginger, ground coriander, cumin, chili powder, paprika, turmeric, and sugar into a large wok or skillet. Pour in the measured water and stir to mix well. Bring to a boil, reduce the heat, and cook, covered, for 8–10 minutes.

Add the mango, coconut milk, and tamarind paste and stir to combine. Bring the mixture back to a boil, then add the shrimp. Reduce the heat and simmer gently for 6–8 minutes.

Tear half of the cilantro leaves into the curry and cook for another 2 minutes, until the shrimp have turned pink and are just cooked through. Season to taste and serve immediately with a boiled rice, garnished with the remaining cilantro.

For chicken & sweet potato curry, simmer the spices in the measured water as above. Omit the mango and shrimp and add 1 small peeled and diced sweet potato and 1 lb diced skinless chicken breasts with the coconut milk and tamarind paste. Bring to a boil, reduce the heat, and simmer gently for 20 minutes, until the chicken is cooked through. Add the cilantro and serve as above. **Calories per serving 454**

scallops with spiced lentils

Calories per serving **451**
Serves **4**
Preparation time **10 minutes**
Cooking time **20–25 minutes**

1 ¼ cup dried **red lentils**,
  rinsed
⅓ cup **olive oil**
2 tablespoons **butter**
1 **onion**, finely chopped
1 **eggplant**, cut into ½ inch
  cubes
1 **garlic clove**, finely chopped
1 tablespoon **curry powder**
1 tablespoon chopped
  parsley, plus extra to garnish
12 cleaned **sea scallops**,
  corals removed (optional)
salt and **black pepper**

Cook the lentils in a saucepan of boiling water according to the package directions. Drain well.

Meanwhile, heat 1 tablespoon of the oil and the butter in a skillet over medium heat, add the onion, and cook slowly for 10 minutes or until golden brown. Transfer with a slotted spoon to a plate and turn the heat up to high. Add another 2 tablespoons of the oil to the pan and sauté the eggplant, in batches, until browned and softened.

Return the onion to the pan with the garlic, curry powder, and cooked lentils and sauté for another minute to warm through. Season with salt and black pepper and stir in the parsley.

Heat another skillet over high heat, then add the remaining oil. Season the scallops with salt and black pepper, put them into the pan and cook for 1 minute on each side or until just cooked through. Serve immediately with the spiced lentils and garnish with parsley leaves.

For scallops with dhal & spinach, cook 1 ¼ cups yellow split pea lentils according to the package directions and drain well. Heat a little vegetable oil in a skillet, add the onion and garlic, omitting the eggplant, and sauté until softened. Add 1 teaspoon curry powder, 1 teaspoon garam masala, and a pinch of turmeric and cook for 1 minute. Add the cooked lentils with a little water or chicken stock or broth to moisten the mixture. Add 1 (1 lb) package baby leaf spinach and stir until wilted. Cook the scallops as above with a light sprinkle of curry powder on each. Serve with the dhal.
Calories per serving 439

malaysian rendang lamb

Calories per serving **455**
Serves **6**
Preparation time **15 minutes**
Cooking time **2¾ hours**

2 tablespoons **sunflower oil**
1 ½ lb **leg of lamb**, butterflied
2 **onions**, finely chopped
1 tablespoon **ground coriander**
1 teaspoon **ground turmeric**
6 **garlic cloves**, crushed
⅓ cup finely chopped **lemon grass**
4–6 **Thai chiles**, chopped
¼ cup finely chopped **fresh cilantro root** and **stem**
1⅔ cups can **reduced-fat coconut milk**
salt and **black pepper**

Heat the oil in a deep, heavy casserole dish or Dutch oven and brown the lamb on both sides for 5–6 minutes.

Put the remaining ingredients into a food processor and blend until smooth. Season well.

Pour the mixture over the lamb and bring to a boil. Cover tightly and cook in a preheated oven, at 300°F, turning the lamb occasionally, for 2½ hours or until the lamb is meltingly tender and most of the liquid has evaporated.

Remove from the oven and let the lamb stand for 10–12 minutes before serving, cut into thick slices.

For winter salad, to serve as an accompaniment to this dish, mix together 3 cups finely shredded green cabbage, 1 carrot, shredded, and 1 red onion, finely sliced. In a separate dish, mix together 3 tablespoons light olive oil and the juice of 1 lemon. Season the dressing well and pour it over the salad mixture. Toss until the salad is thoroughly coated in the dressing and serve. **Calories per serving 131**

malaysian scallop & shrimp curry

Calories per serving **456**
Serves **4**
Preparation time **20 minutes**
Cooking time **20–25 minutes**

1 tablespoon **chili powder**
1 teaspoon **ground coriander**
2 teaspoons **ground cumin**
2 **garlic cloves**, crushed
1 **onion**, finely chopped
⅓ cup finely chopped
   lemon grass
1 teaspoon **grated galangal**
   or **fresh ginger root**
1 tablespoon **grated**
   palm sugar
½ teaspoon **shrimp paste**
2 tablespoons finely chopped
   unroasted peanuts
2½ cups **coconut milk**
2 cups trimmed **green bean**
   halfs
1 lb **raw jumbo shrimp**
1 lb **raw scallops**

To garnish
Thai basil leaves
4 teaspoons chopped
   unroasted peanuts
finely chopped **fresh**
   red chiles

Put the chili powder, ground coriander, cumin, garlic, onion, lemon grass, galangal or ginger, palm sugar, shrimp paste, peanuts, and coconut milk into a food processor and process until fairly smooth.

Put a large wok over high heat and add the spice mixture. Bring to a boil, reduce the heat, and simmer gently, uncovered, for 12–15 minutes, stirring occasionally.

Add the green beans, shrimp, and scallops and bring back to a boil. Reduce the heat and simmer gently for 6–8 minutes or until the shrimp and scallops are cooked through.

Remove from the heat and sprinkle over some Thai basil leaves, chopped peanuts, and chopped red chiles before serving.

For spicy squid & shrimp, add 11½ oz squid rings instead of the scallops and proceed as above. Serve with rice sticks or cellophane noodles instead of rice. **Calories per serving 392**

tindora & lentil curry

Calories per serving **463**
Serves **4**
Preparation time **15 minutes**
Cooking time **35 minutes**

⅔ cup **dried green lentils**, rinsed
1 tablespoon **peanut oil**
1 teaspoon **ground turmeric**
2 teaspoons **garam masala** (see page 80)
1 teaspoon **cumin seeds**
1 teaspoon **nigella seeds**
1 **fresh red chile,** finely chopped
1 **fresh green chile,** finely chopped
3 large **tomatoes**, chopped
8 oz **tindora (ivy gourd)**, rinsed and trimmed, or
  1 **zucchini** or **yellow squash**, cut into chunks
2 tablespoons packed **palm sugar** or **brown sugar**
1 tablespoon **tamarind paste**
⅔ cup **boiling water**
4 warm **chapatis**
salt and **black pepper**

Cook the lentils in a saucepan of boiling water for 20 minutes, until soft. Drain well.

Meanwhile, heat the oil in a large saucepan and sauté the turmeric, garam masala, cumin seeds, and nigella seeds for 1–2 minutes or until the spices are sizzling. Add the chopped chiles, tomatoes, lentils, and tindora, zucchini, or squash and bring to a boil. Cover the pan, reduce the heat, and simmer gently for 10 minutes, stirring occasionally.

Mix the sugar and tamarind paste with the boiling water and add to the pan. Stir well and simmer for another 5 minutes. Season to taste and serve with 1 chapati per person and a green mango and red onion salad.

For green mango & red onion salad, to serve as an accompaniment, peel and pit 1 small green mango and finely shred the flesh. Mix with 1 small finely chopped red onion and a handful of cilantro leaves. Cover and chill until required. **Calories per serving 36**

yellow salmon curry

Calories per serving **466**
Serves **4**
Preparation time **15 minutes**
Cooking time **25–30 minutes**

3 **garlic cloves**, finely grated
2 **fresh green chiles**, seeded
   and finely chopped
2 teaspoons peeled and finely
   grated **fresh ginger root**
1 tablespoon **peanut oil**
1 **onion**, finely chopped
1 tablespoon **ground turmeric**
1 cup **reduced-fat
   coconut milk**
1 cup **water**
2 **potatoes**, peeled and diced
4 thick **salmon steaks** (about
   6 oz each)
2 **tomatoes**, coarsely chopped
salt
chopped **fresh cilantro
   leaves**, to garnish

Pound the garlic, chiles, and ginger with a mortar and pestle until you have a smooth paste.

Heat the oil in a large, nonstick wok or saucepan over medium heat. Add the paste and stir-fry for 2–3 minutes, then add the onion and turmeric. Stir-fry for another 2–3 minutes, until fragrant.

Stir in the coconut milk, measured water, and the potatoes. Bring to a boil, reduce the heat to low, and simmer gently for 10–12 minutes, stirring occasionally.

Season the fish with salt and add to the pan with the tomatoes. Bring the mixture back to a boil and simmer gently for 6–8 minutes, until the fish is cooked through. Remove from the heat and garnish with chopped cilantro.

For yellow mussel curry, replace the salmon with 2 lb mussels, which have been scrubbed and debearded. Cover the pan and cook over high heat for 6–8 minutes or until the mussels have opened, discarding any that do not. Remove from the heat and garnish with chopped cilantro. **Calories per serving 212**

chicken, okra, & red lentil dhal

Calories per serving **466**
Serves **4**
Preparation time **15 minutes**
Cooking time **45 minutes**

2 teaspoons **ground cumin**
1 teaspoon **ground coriander**
½ teaspoon **cayenne pepper**
¼ teaspoon **ground turmeric**
1 lb skinless, boneless
   chicken thighs, cut into
   large pieces
2 tablespoons **peanut oil**
1 **onion**, sliced
2 garlic **cloves**, crushed
¼ cup peeled and finely
   chopped **fresh ginger root**
3 cups **water**
1½ cups **dried red lentils**,
   rinsed
16 **okra pods** (about 7 oz)
small handful of **fresh cilantro**
   leaves, chopped
salt
lime wedges, to garnish

Mix the cumin, coriander, cayenne, and turmeric and toss with the chicken pieces.

Heat the oil in a large saucepan. Cook the chicken pieces, in batches, until deep golden brown, transferring each batch to a plate. Add the onion to the pan and sauté for 5 minutes, until golden brown. Stir in the garlic and ginger and cook for another 1 minute.

Return the chicken to the pan and add the measured water. Bring to a boil, reduce the heat, and simmer gently, covered, for 20 minutes, until the chicken is cooked through. Add the lentils and cook for 5 minutes.

Stir in the okra, cilantro, and a little salt and cook for another 5 minutes, until the lentils are tender but not completely pulpy. Serve in shallow bowls with lime wedges.

For chicken, zucchini & chile dhal, follow the main recipe but replace the okra with 3 medium zucchini, thinly sliced. For a hotter flavor, add 1 thinly sliced medium-strength red chile with the garlic and ginger. **Calories per serving 471**

spicy lentils & chickpeas

Calories per serving **466**
Serves **4**
Preparation time **15 minutes**
Cooking time **about**
   35 minutes

1 tablespoon **peanut oil**
1 **onion**, finely chopped
2 **garlic cloves**, thinly sliced
2 **celery sticks**, diced
1 **green bell pepper**, cored,
   seeded, and chopped
¾ cup **dried red lentils**, rinsed
2 teaspoons **garam masala**
   (see page 80)
1 teaspoon **cumin seeds**
½ teaspoon **hot chili powder**
1 teaspoon **ground coriander**
2 tablespoons **tomato paste**
3 cups hot **vegetable stock**
   or **broth**
1⅔ cups rinsed and drained,
   canned **chickpeas**
salt and **black pepper**
2 tablespoons chopped **fresh**
   cilantro, to garnish
¾ cup boiled **brown rice** per
   person, to serve

Heat the oil in a heavy saucepan over medium heat, add the onion, garlic, celery, and green bell pepper, and sauté gently for 10–12 minutes or until softened and beginning to brown.

Stir in the lentils and spices and cook for 2–3 minutes, stirring frequently. Add the tomato paste, stock or broth, and chickpeas and bring to a boil. Reduce the heat, cover, and simmer gently for about 20 minutes or until the lentils collapse. Season with salt and black pepper to taste.

Ladle into bowls and sprinkle with the cilantro. Serve immediately with boiled brown rice and cooling, spiced yogurt (see below).

For cooling, spiced yogurt, to serve as an accompaniment, mix together 1 cup fat-free plain yogurt, 2 tablespoons lemon juice, and ½ teaspoon of garam masala in a small bowl. Fold in ½ a small, seeded and grated cucumber, then season with salt and black pepper to taste. Serve sprinkled with 1 tablespoon chopped cilantro. **Calories per serving 33**

mango curry

Calories per serving **469**
Serves **4**
Preparation time **10 minutes**
Cooking time **8–10 minutes**

1 tablespoon **vegetable oil**
1 teaspoon **mustard seeds**
1 **onion**, halved and thinly
  sliced
15–20 **curry leaves, fresh**
  or **dried**
½ teaspoon **dried red pepper**
  flakes
1 teaspoon peeled and grated
  fresh ginger root
1 **green chile,** seeded and
  sliced
1 teaspoon **ground turmeric**
3 ripe **mangoes**, peeled,
  pitted, and thinly sliced
1⅔ cups **plain yogurt**,
  lightly beaten
salt
1 warm **chapati** per person,
  to serve

Heat the oil in a large saucepan until hot, add the mustard seeds, onion, curry leaves, and red pepper flakes and sauté, stirring, for 4–5 minutes or until the onion is lightly browned.

Add the ginger and chile and sauté, stirring, for 1 minute, then add the turmeric and stir to mix well.

Remove the pan from the heat, add the mangoes and yogurt, and stir continuously until well mixed. Season to taste with salt.

Return the pan to low heat and heat through for 1 minute, stirring continuously. (Do not let it boil or the curry will curdle.) Serve immediately with 1 warm chapati per person.

For eggplant & pea curry, heat 1 tablespoon sunflower oil in a large skillet until hot, then add 3 peeled and cubed red-skinned or Yukon gold potatoes, 1 eggplant, cut into small chunks, 1 cup frozen peas, 2 finely sliced onions, 2 crushed garlic cloves, 1 tablespoon ginger paste, and 2 tablespoons medium curry powder. Stir-fry for 3–4 minutes or until the onion has softened and is turning golden brown, then pour in 2½ cups chicken or vegetable stock or broth and cook for 10–15 minutes or until the stock or broth has reduced. Stir in ⅔ cup reduced-fat crème fraîche or Greek-style yogurt and serve with ½ a large naan per person. **Calories per serving 473**

green chicken curry

Calories per serving **469**
Serves **4**
Preparation time **15 minutes**
Cooking time **30–35 minutes**

1 tablespoon **sunflower oil**
3 tablespoons **Thai green
  curry paste** (see right)
2 **fresh green chiles**, finely
  chopped
1½ lb boneless, skinless
  chicken thighs, cut into
  bite-size pieces
1⅔ cups **coconut milk**
1 cup **chicken stock** or **broth**
6 **lime leaves**
2 tablespoons **Thai fish sauce**
1 tablespoon **grated palm
  sugar**
7 oz **pea eggplants**, or
  1 **standard eggplant**, diced
1 cup trimmed **green beans**
⅓ cup rinsed and drained,
  canned **bamboo shoots**
large handful of **Thai basil
  leaves**
large handful of **fresh cilantro
  leaves**
¼ cup **lime juice**

Heat the oil in a large, nonstick wok or saucepan and add the curry paste and chiles. Stir-fry for 2–3 minutes and then add the chicken. Stir and cook for 5–6 minutes or until the chicken is sealed and lightly browned.

Stir in the coconut milk, stock, lime leaves, fish sauce, palm sugar, and pea eggplants. Simmer, uncovered for 10–15 minutes, stirring occasionally.

Add the green beans and bamboo shoots and continue to simmer for 6–8 minutes.

Remove from the heat and stir in the herbs and lime juice. Serve ladled into warmed bowls.

For homemade Thai green curry paste, blend the following ingredients to a smooth paste in a food processor: 4–6 long green chiles, chopped, 2 tablespoons chopped garlic, 2 tablespoons chopped lemon grass stalks, 4 shallots, finely chopped, 1 tablespoon finely chopped galangal or fresh ginger root, 2 teaspoons finely chopped lime leaves, 2 teaspoons ground coriander, 2 teaspoons ground cumin, 1 teaspoon white peppercorns, 2 teaspoons shrimp paste, and 1 tablespoon peanut oil. Store in an airtight container in the refrigerator for up to one month. **Calories per tablespoon 22**

squash, carrot, & mango tagine

Calories per serving **474**
Serves **4**
Preparation time **15 minutes**
Cooking time **35–40 minutes**

2 tablespoons **olive oil**
1 large **onion**, cut into large
  chunks
3 **garlic cloves**, finely chopped
1 **butternut squash**, peeled,
  seeded, and cubed
2 small **carrots**, peeled and
  cut into thick batons
½ (1 inch) **cinnamon stick**
½ teaspoon **turmeric**
¼ teaspoon **cayenne pepper**
  (optional)
½ teaspoon **ground cumin**
1 teaspoon **paprika**
pinch of **saffron threads**
1 tablespoon **tomato paste**
3 cups hot **vegetable stock**
  or **broth**
1 **mango**, peeled, pitted, and
  cut into 1 inch chunks
salt and **black pepper**
2 tablespoons chopped **fresh
cilantro**, to garnish

Heat the oil in a large, heavy saucepan over medium heat, add the onion, and cook for 5 minutes or until beginning to soften. Add the garlic, squash, carrots, and spices and sauté gently for another 5 minutes.

Stir in the tomato paste, then pour in the stock or broth and season with salt and black pepper to taste. Cover and simmer gently for 20–25 minutes or until the vegetables are tender. Stir in the mango and simmer gently for another 5 minutes.

Ladle the tagine into serving bowls and sprinkle with the cilantro and serve with steamed couscous.

For spicy squash & carrot soup, make the tagine as above, adding an extra 1 cup vegetable stock or broth. Once the vegetables are tender, put into a food processor or blender and blend until smooth. Ladle into bowls and serve sprinkled with the chopped cilantro. **Calories per serving 253**

salmon curry with tomato salad

Calories per serving **477**
Serves **2**
Preparation time **10 minutes**
Cooking time **20 minutes**

1 teaspoon **vegetable oil**
1 **small onion**, sliced
1 **garlic clove**, chopped
1 teaspoon **tandoori spice mix**
1 **cinnamon stick**
8 **cherry tomatoes**, halved
¼ cup **reduced-fat crème fraîche** or **Greek-style yogurt**
grated zest and juice of ½ **lime**
6 oz **skinless salmon fillet**, cut into chunks
1 tablespoon chopped **mint**
1 tablespoon chopped **fresh cilantro**

Tomato & onion salad
2 small **ripe tomatoes**, thinly sliced
1 **small red onion**, finely sliced
handful of **fresh cilantro**, chopped
1 teaspoon **lemon juice**

Heat the oil in a small skillet. Add the onion and garlic and sauté for 2–3 minutes, until softened. Stir in the spice mix and cinnamon stick and sauté for another minute. Add the tomatoes, crème fraîche or yogurt, and lime zest and juice, and heat for a minute.

Put the salmon into an ovenproof dish. Spoon the sauce over the fish, cover the dish tightly with aluminum foil and cook in a preheated oven, at 400°F, for 15–20 minutes or until the salmon is just cooked.

Meanwhile, make the salad by tossing together the tomatoes, onion, and cilantro. Dress with lemon juice.

Serve the salmon with the tomato and onion salad.

For paneer curry, prepare the sauce as above. Cut 5 oz paneer into cubes and put the pieces into an ovenproof dish. Pour the sauce over the paneer, making sure the cubes are evenly coated, cover with aluminum foil, and cook as above. Serve with the tomato and onion salad. **Calories per serving 409**

vegetable & rice noodle laksa

Calories per serving **479**
Serves **4**
Preparation time **20 minutes**
Cooking time **40 minutes**

1 tablespoon **peanut oil**
2 tablespoons chopped **garlic**
1 tablespoon peeled and finely
   chopped **fresh ginger root**
2 **fresh red chiles**, sliced
2 **onions**, finely sliced
¼ cup l**aksa curry paste**
1¼ cups **vegetable stock**
   or **broth**
7 oz **dried rice noodles**
1⅔ cups **reduced-fat**
   coconut milk
1 tablespoon **chili bean sauce**
1 teaspoon **agave syrup**
½ cup **bean sprouts**

To serve
4 **scallions**, finely sliced
1 **fresh red chile,** seeded
   and thinly shredded
½ cup finely chopped **fresh**
   cilantro leaves
2 **eggs**, hard-boiled, peeled,
   and halved
⅔ cup **roasted skinless**
   peanuts, coarsely chopped

Heat a wok or large skillet over high heat. Add the oil and, when it is starting to smoke, reduce the heat and add the garlic, ginger, chiles, and onion. Stir-fry for 5 minutes. Add the curry paste and stock or broth, reduce the heat to low, cove,r and simmer for 20 minutes.

Meanwhile, soak the rice noodles in a bowl of warm water for 20 minutes, until tender, or according to the package directions. Drain well.

Add the coconut milk to the simmering liquid in the pan. Season with the chili bean sauce and agave syrup, and add the bean sprouts. Continue simmering for another 15 minutes.

Divide the noodles among 4 warm serving bowls and ladle the coconut broth over the top. Serve immediately with the scallions, chile, cilantro, eggs, and peanuts in individual bowls, from which diners can help themselves.

For spicy vegetable & rice noodle stir-fry, heat 1 tablespoon peanut oil in a large wok over medium heat. Add 1 sliced onion, 3 thinly sliced garlic cloves, 1 teaspoon grated ginger, and 2 sliced red chiles, and stir-fry for 2–3 minutes. Add 1 (12 oz) package of prepared stir-fry vegetables and 10 oz fresh rice noodles. Stir-fry for 3–4 minutes or until piping hot. Stir in 3 tablespoons light soy and 3 tablespoons sweet chili sauce, toss to mix well, and serve immediately. **Calories per serving 226**

asian lamb burgers

Calories per serving **480**
Serves **4**
Preparation time **20 minutes**
Cooking time **30 minutes**

2 **garlic cloves**, crushed
1 **lemon grass** stalk, finely
  chopped
¼ cup grated **fresh
  ginger root**
large handful of **fresh cilantro,**
  coarsely chopped
1 **hot red chile,** seeded and
  thinly sliced
1 lb **lean ground lamb**
2 tablespoons **oil**
1 **small cucumber**
1 bunch **scallions**
7 oz **bok choy**
3 tablespoons packed
  light brown sugar
finely grated zest and juice
  of 2 **limes**
2 tablespoons **Thai fish sauce**
⅓ cup **roasted peanuts**
salt

Blend the garlic, lemon grass, ginger, cilantro, chile, and a little salt in a food processor to make a thick paste. Add the lamb and blend until mixed. Turn out onto the work surface and divide the mixture into 4 pieces. Roll each into a ball and flatten into a burger shape.

Heat the oil in a sturdy roasting pan and cook the burgers on both sides to sear. Transfer to a preheated oven, at 400°F, and cook, uncovered, for 25 minutes, until the burgers are cooked through.

Meanwhile, peel the cucumber and cut in half lengthwise. Scoop out the seeds with a teaspoon and discard. Cut the cucumber into thin, diagonal slices. Slice the scallions diagonally. Coarsely shred the bok choy; keep the white parts separate from the green.

Using a large metal spoon, drain off all but about 2 tablespoons fat from the roasting pan. Arrange all the vegetables except the green parts of the bok choy around the meat and toss them gently in the pan juices. Return to the oven, uncovered, for 5 minutes.

Mix together the sugar, lime zest and juice, and fish sauce. Sprinkle the bok choy greens and peanuts into the roasting pan and drizzle with half the dressing.

Toss the salad ingredients together gently. Transfer the lamb and salad to serving plates and drizzle with the remaining dressing.

For chicken burgers, use ground chicken instead of the lamb. Replace the bok choy with shredded collard greens and peanuts with salted cashew nuts. **Calories per serving 400**

crab & coconut chowder

Calories per serving **481**
Serves **4**
Preparation time **15 minutes**
Cooking time **50 minutes**

2 tablespoons **butter**
1 tablespoon **vegetable oil**
1 large **onion**, chopped
7 oz **lean pork belly**,
  finely diced
2 **garlic cloves**, crushed
⅔ cup **dry white wine**
¾ cup canned **diced
  tomatoes**
1⅔ cups **reduced-fat
  coconut milk**
1 teaspoon **medium
  curry paste**
3 **red-skinned** or **Yukon gold
  potatoes**, peeled and diced
10 oz **white** and **brown
  crabmeat**
3 tablespoons **heavy cream**
salt and **black pepper**

Melt the butter with the oil in a large saucepan and gently sauté the onion and pork, stirring, for about 10 minutes, until lightly browned. Stir in the garlic and sauté for 1 minute. Lift the pork out with a slotted spoon onto a plate.

Add the wine to the pan, bring to a boil, and boil for about 5 minutes, until slightly reduced.

Return the pork to the pan, add the tomatoes, coconut milk, curry paste, and potatoes, and heat until simmering. Reduce the heat to its lowest setting, cover, and cook for 30 minutes.

Stir in the crabmeat and cream, heat through thoroughly, and season to taste with salt and black pepper. Serve hot with crusty bread, if desired.

For halibut & corn chowder, melt 2 tablespoons butter in a large saucepan and gently sauté 1 chopped onion and 1 chopped celery stick. Stir in 2 teaspoons crushed coriander seeds, ¼ teaspoon ground turmeric, 2½ cups milk, and 2 cups fish or chicken stock or broth. Bring just to a boil, then reduce the heat to its lowest setting. Stir in 4 peeled and diced red-skinned or Yukon gold potatoes and 1¼ lb diced skinless halibut, red snapper, cod, or smoked haddock. Cover and cook gently for 10 minutes, then stir in 1¼ cups corn kernels and cook for another 10 minutes. Season to taste with black pepper and serve. **Calories per serving 428**

lime, ginger, & cilantro chicken

Calories per serving **482**
Serves **4**
Preparation time
5–10 minutes
Cooking time **50 minutes**

3 **limes**
½ inch piece **fresh ginger root**, peeled and finely grated
¼ cup finely chopped **fresh cilantro**, plus extra leaves to serve
2 teaspoons **vegetable oil**
4 **chicken legs**
¾ cup steamed **rice** per person, to serve
salt

Finely grate the zest of 2 of the limes and halve these limes. Mix the zest with the ginger and cilantro in a nonmetallic bowl and stir in 1 teaspoon of the oil to make a coarse paste.

Carefully lift the skin from the chicken legs and push the ginger paste under it. Pull the skin back into place, then cut 3–4 slashes in the thickest parts of the legs and brush with the remaining oil.

Put the legs in a roasting pan, flesh side down, with the halved limes and cook in a preheated oven, at 425°F, for 45–50 minutes, basting occasionally. The legs are cooked when the meat comes away from the bone and the juices run clear when the thickest part of the leg is pierced with the tip of a sharp knife.

Spoon the rice into small bowls to mold, then turn onto serving plates. Add the chicken legs, squeeze with the roasted lime, and sprinkle with cilantro leaves. Serve immediately with the remaining lime, cut into wedges, and rice.

For Mediterranean chicken, replace the ginger paste with a red pesto made by blending 6 sun-dried tomatoes, 1 tablespoon pine nuts, ½ clove chopped garlic, 1 tablespoon chopped basil, 1 teaspoon grated lemon zest, 1 tablespoon lemon juice, 2 tablespoons olive oil, and 1 tablespoon grated Parmesan cheese. **Calories per serving 499**

caribbean lamb stoba

Calories per serving **483**
Serves **4**
Preparation time **25 minutes**
Cooking time **1¾ hours**

1 tablespoon **peanut oil**
1½ lb **lean lamb**, cubed
2 **onions**, finely chopped
2 teaspoons finely grated
   fresh ginger root
1 **scotch bonnet chile**,
   thinly sliced
1 **red bell pepper**, cored,
   seeded, and coarsely
   chopped
2 teaspoons **ground allspice**
3 teaspoons **ground cumin**
1 **cinnamon stick**
pinch of grated **nutmeg**
1⅔ cups canned **diced**
   tomatoes
2 cups **cherry tomatoes**
finely grated zest and juice
   of 2 **limes**
⅓ cup firmly packed **light**
   brown sugar
1⅓ cups fresh or frozen **peas**
salt and **black pepper**

Heat half the oil in a large saucepan. Brown the lamb, in batches, for 3–4 minutes. Remove with a slotted spoon and set aside.

Heat the remaining oil in the saucepan and add the onion, ginger, chile, red bell pepper, and spices. Stir-fry for 3–4 minutes, then add the lamb with the canned and cherry tomatoes, lime zest and juice, and sugar. Season and bring to a boil. Reduce the heat, cover tightly, and simmer gently for 1½ hours or until the lamb is tender.

Stir in the peas 5 minutes before serving on warmed plates with rice.

mustard, mango, & yogurt curry

Calories per serving **491**
Serves **4**
Preparation time **20 minutes**
Cooking time **about
  20 minutes**

3¾ cups grated **fresh
  coconut**
3–4 **fresh green chiles**,
  coarsely chopped
1 tablespoon **cumin seeds**
2 cups **water**
3 firm, ripe **mangoes**, peeled,
  pitted, and cubed
1 teaspoon **ground turmeric**
1 teaspoon **chili powder**
1¼ cups **fat-free plain yogurt,**
  lightly whisked
1 tablespoon **peanut oil**
2 teaspoons **black mustard
  seeds**
3–4 **hot dried red chiles**
10–12 **curry leaves**

Put the coconut, green chiles, and cumin seeds into a
food processor with half the measured water and blend
to a fine paste.

Put the mangoes into a heavy saucepan with the
turmeric, chili powder, and the remaining measured
water. Bring to a boil, add the coconut paste, and stir
to mix well. Cover and simmer over medium heat for
10–12 minutes, stirring occasionally, until the mixture
becomes fairly thick.

Add the yogurt and heat gently, stirring, until just
warmed through. Do not let the mixture come to a boil
or it will curdle. Remove from the heat and keep warm.

Heat the oil in a small saucepan over medium-high
heat. Add the mustard seeds and as soon as they begin
to "pop" (after a few seconds), add the dried chiles and
curry leaves. Stir-fry for a few seconds until the chiles
darken. Stir the spice mixture into the mango curry and
serve immediately.

For spicy mango & mint salad, peel, pit, and cube
4 ripe mangoes. Put into a serving dish with ½ thinly
sliced red onion, 12 halved cherry tomatoes, and a large
handful of mint leaves. Make a dressing by whisking
1 cup fat-free plain yogurt with the juice of 1 lime,
1 teaspoon agave syrup, and 1 finely diced red chile.
Season, drizzle the dressing over the salad, toss to mix
well, and serve. **Calories per serving 204**

mixed bean kedgeree

Calories per serving **497**
Serves **4**
Preparation time **10 minutes**
Cooking time **15–20 minutes**

1 tablespoon **olive oil**
1 **onion**, chopped
2 tablespoons **mild curry powder**
1¼ cups **long-grain rice**
3 cups **vegetable stock** or **broth**
4 **eggs**
4 cups rinsed and drained, canned **mixed beans**, such as kidney beans, pinto beans, and chickpeas
⅔ cup **fat-free fromage blanc** or **Greek-style yogurt**
salt and **black pepper**
2 **tomatoes**, finely chopped, to garnish
flat leaf parsley, to garnish

Heat the oil in a saucepan, add the onion, and cook until soft. Stir in the curry powder and rice. Add the stock or broth and season to taste with salt and black pepper. Bring to a boil, then reduce the heat, cover, and simmer, stirring occasionally, for 10–15 minutes, until all the stock or broth has been absorbed and the rice is tender.

Meanwhile, put the eggs in a saucepan of cold water and bring to a boil. Cook for 10 minutes, then plunge into cold water to cool. Shell the eggs, then cut them into wedges.

Stir through the beans and fromage blanc or yogurt and cook briefly over low heat to heat through. Serve garnished with the eggs, tomatoes, and parsley.

turkish lamb & spinach curry

Calories per serving **497**
Serves **4**
Preparation time **20 minutes**
Cooking time **2 hours**

¼ cup **sunflower oil**
1 ¼ lb **boneless shoulder
   of lamb**, cut into bite-size
   pieces
1 **onion**, finely chopped
3 **garlic cloves**, crushed
1 teaspoon **ground ginger**
2 teaspoons **ground turmeric**
large pinch of **grated nutmeg**
¼ cup **golden raisins**
1 teaspoon **ground cinnamon**
1 teaspoon **paprika**
1 ⅔ cups canned **diced
   tomatoes**
1 ¼ cups **lamb stock** or **broth**
1 (12 oz) package **baby
   leaf spinach**
salt and **black pepper**
Greek-style or **plain yogurt**,
   whisked, to serve (optional)

Heat half the oil in a large, heavy saucepan and brown the lamb, in batches, for 3–4 minutes. Remove with a slotted spoon and set aside.

Heat the remaining oil in the pan and add the onion, garlic, ginger, turmeric, nutmeg, golden raisins, cinnamon, and paprika. Stir-fry for 1–2 minutes, then add the lamb. Stir-fry for another 2–3 minutes, then add the tomatoes and stock or broth. Season well and bring to a boil.

Reduce the heat, cover tightly, and simmer gently (using a heat diffuser, if possible) for 1 ½ hours.

Add the spinach, in batches, until it is all wilted, cover, and cook for another 10–12 minutes, stirring occasionally. Remove from the heat and serve drizzled with whisked yogurt, if desired.

For Turkish lamb & eggplant curry, use a large eggplant instead of the spinach. Cut the eggplant into bite-size chunks and sauté it in oil until light golden brown, along with the lamb. You may need to add a little more oil to cook the eggplant. **Calories per serving 475**

coconut lamb curry

Calories per serving **497**
Serves **4**
Preparation time **15 minutes**
Cooking time **about 2 hours**

2 tablespoons **sunflower oil**
1 **onion**, thinly sliced
2 teaspoons grated **fresh ginger root**
2 teaspoons **crushed garlic**
1 teaspoon **ground cinnamon**
20 **curry leaves**
2 tablespoons **mild curry powder**
1 tablespoon **ground coriander**
1 teaspoon **ground turmeric**
1 teaspoon **chili powder**
1¼ lb **boneless lamb**, cut into chunks
1⅔ cups **coconut milk**
1 cup **vegetable stock** or **broth**
1¼ cups grated **fresh coconut**
⅓ cup chopped **fresh cilantro**
salt and **black pepper**

Heat the oil in a large, heavy saucepan.

Add the onion and stir-fry over medium heat for 4–5 minutes. Stir in the ginger, garlic, cinnamon, curry leaves, curry powder, ground coriander, turmeric, and chili powder. Stir-fry for 2–3 minutes and then add the lamb.

Stir-fry for 2–3 minutes and then stir in the coconut milk and stock or broth. Bring to a boil, season well, and cover tightly. Cook over a low heat (using a heat diffuser, if possible), stirring occasionally, for 1½–2 hours or until the lamb is tender. Remove from the heat and sprinkle over the grated coconut and chopped fresh cilantro before serving.

For coconut chicken curry, use 1½ lb skinless chicken thighs on the bone instead of the lamb, and reduce the cooking time to 1–1½ hours. After 1 hour add ½ small cauliflower, cut into florets, and 4 carrots, peeled, halved lengthwise, and sliced. Sprinkle in ⅓ cup golden raisins or raisins, if desired. **Calories per serving 495**

thai green pork curry

Calories per serving **498**
Serves **4**
Preparation time **10 minutes**
Cooking time **20 minutes**

2 tablespoons **olive oil**
4 boneless **pork cutlets**, cut
  into bite-size pieces
2 tablespoons **Thai green
  curry paste** (see page 208)
1⅔ cups **coconut milk**
1 cup trimmed **green beans**
1⅔ cups drained, rinsed,
  and halved, canned **water
  chestnuts**
juice of **1 lime**, or to taste
1 handful of **fresh cilantro
  leaves**

Heat the oil in a large saucepan, add the pork, and cook, stirring, for 3–4 minutes, until browned all over. Add the curry paste and cook, stirring, for 1 minute, until fragrant.

Add the coconut milk, stir, and reduce the heat to a gentle simmer. Cook for 10 minutes, then add the beans and water chestnuts. Cook for another 3 minutes.

Remove from the heat, add lime juice to taste, and stir through the cilantro. Serve immediately with boiled rice.

For Thai red pork curry, replace the Thai green curry paste with Thai red curry paste. To prepare your own Thai red curry paste, put 10 large red chiles, 2 teaspoons coriander seeds, 2 inch piece of fresh ginger root, peeled and finely chopped, 1 finely chopped lemon grass stalk, 4 halved garlic cloves, 1 coarsely chopped shallot, 1 teaspoon lime juice, and 2 tablespoons peanut oil in a food processor or blender and process to a thick paste. Alternatively, pound the ingredients together, using a mortar and pestle. Transfer the paste to an airtight container; it can be stored in the refrigerator for up to 3 weeks. **Calories per serving 498**

kheema mutter

Calories per serving **499**
Serves **4**
Preparation time **20 minutes**
Cooking time **1½–2 hours**

2 tablespoons **sunflower oil**
1 **large onion**, finely chopped
3 **garlic cloves**, crushed
1 teaspoon **finely grated
 fresh ginger root**
3–4 **fresh green chiles**,
 seeded and finely sliced
1 tablespoon **cumin seeds**
3 tablespoons **hot curry paste**
1½ lb **ground beef**
1⅔ cups canned **diced
 tomatoes**
1 teaspoon **sugar**
¼ cup **tomato paste**
¼ cup **coconut cream** or
 coconut milk
1⅔ cups **fresh** or **frozen peas**
salt and **black pepper**
large handful of chopped **fresh
 cilantro**, to garnish

Heat the oil in a large, heavy saucepan and add the onion. Cook over low heat for 15–20 minutes, until softened and just turning light golden brown.

Add the garlic, ginger, chile, cumin seeds, and curry paste and stir-fry over high heat for 1–2 minutes.

Add the ground beef and stir-fry for 3–4 minutes. Stir in the tomatoes, sugar, and tomato paste and bring to a boil. Season well, cover, and reduce the heat to low. Cook for 1–1½ hours, until the meat is tender.

Pour in the coconut cream or milk and add the peas 10 minutes before the end of cooking time. Garnish with the chopped cilantro and serve lime slices and red chiles as well as rice or a naan, if desired.

index

acknowledgments

Commissioning Editor: Eleanor Maxfield
Design: Jeremy Tilston & Jaz Bahra
Assistant Production Manager: Caroline Alberti

Photography copyright © Octopus Publishing Group/
Frank Adam 33. Stephen Conroy 1, 2–3, 6–7, 14, 15,
18–19, 30, 49, 53, 55, 61–62, 67, 69, 71, 91, 93, 103,
107, 108-109, 113, 119, 127, 133, 137, 139, 145, 147,
151, 153, 155, 161, 169, 173, 175, 177, 179, 183, 185,
191, 195, 197, 209, 213, 221, 223, 227, 229, 231,
233, 235. Will Heap 4–5, 8, 10, 11, 16, 25, 35, 37, 39,
43, 45, 47, 57, 59, 65, 73, 75, 79, 81, 85, 97, 105, 111,
115, 121, 123, 125, 131, 135, 143, 149, 171, 181,
187, 189, 201, 207, 215, 225. William Lingwood 99.
Neil Mersh 89. David Munns 117, 157, 193.
Lis Parsons 13, 137, 141, 165, 166-167, 203, 217.
Gareth Sambidge 27, 41. William Shaw 83, 101, 205,
211, 219. William Reavell 23, 29, 31, 51, 77, 129, 159,
163. Ian Wallace 87, 95, 199.